Management for Professionals

More information about this series at http://www.springer.com/series/10101

Sathit Parniangtong

Supply Management

Strategic Sourcing

 Springer

Sathit Parniangtong
CMBT Strategy and Management Consulting
Bangkok, Thailand

ISSN 2192-8096 ISSN 2192-810X (electronic)
Management for Professionals
ISBN 978-981-10-9431-6 ISBN 978-981-10-1723-0 (eBook)
DOI 10.1007/978-981-10-1723-0

This Springer imprint is published by Springer Nature
The registered company is Springer Science+Business Media Singapore Pte Ltd.

Preface

For many businesses, the quest to increase shareholder value is a never-ending journey. As companies strive to generate a superior financial performance, they are scrambling for new ways to increase a customer's willingness to pay while lowering costs. Profit is king. This makes it much harder to create customer value and lower costs simultaneously. What's worse, once a firm achieves an advantage, others find ways to take it away. It's getting increasingly difficult to differentiate products, including Intel's chip technology, Wal-Mart's new store formats or Starbucks' premium coffee in an inviting environment. Many imitators can quickly match any "unique" product or service. Should a company then focus on bear-hugging each customer? Sorry, everyone's doing that. What about finding new markets instead? Honestly, is there any market a company's competitors cannot and will not follow? All of these leading companies, which dominate their fields, face new challenges to stay ahead of the pack and boost profitability.

As new sources of value creation are getting scarce, many leading companies are looking beyond the four walls of their operations for new sources of value creation. By looking downstream, leading companies begin to realize that long and lasting relationships with existing customers presents a promising source of profit that is difficult to imitate. Many firms are rushing to learn more about their customers with the use of Customer Relationship Management (CRM) to sell more products to existing customers. Looking upstream, leading companies are looking to suppliers as new sources of value creation.

For years, suppliers represented cost centers, and managing them was all about hard-nosed bargaining. They were a group of sellers who were untrustworthy and deserved to be treated as adversaries. Now, many companies have found that a more robust relationship with certain suppliers is better for the bottom line than a more aggressive approach.

So, how can a company forge a productive relationship with its suppliers? This book takes a process approach of identifying, evaluating, selecting, managing and developing suppliers to create more value for customers, which should in turn create more value to shareholders. The book begins by outlining the mental shift necessary to build robust relationships with suppliers. This includes:

- The relationship that shifts from an emphasis on cost reduction to enhancing each other's competitiveness.

- A strategic procurement process that takes a team-based and cross-functional approach to developing a sourcing strategy for each purchasing category.
- The total-cost-of-ownership concept to facilitate both sides to pinpoint areas for achieving a win-win outcome that goes beyond price.
- The negotiation process that focuses on taking costs out of the supply chain, instead of from suppliers.

The second part of this book details strategic sourcing methodology: a step-by-step approach for creating productive relationships with key suppliers. The methodology consists of four distinct stages, from an expenditure category analysis (a purview of total spending), category strategy formulation (assessing the strategic implications of expenditure categories and procurement options), supplier strategy formulation (determining how suppliers should select and maintain solid relationships with suppliers) and fact-based negotiation (a systematic approach for business negotiations). Illustrations and examples from the author's experience are provided throughout.

The third part of this book provides details of a comprehensive process developed to arm the negotiation team with all facts necessary to reach desired outcomes. This detailed step-by-step process consists of negotiation strategy and case building; supplier response and positioning; negotiation planning, discussions and resolution; and supplier evaluation. In addition, the book highlights "best practices" in strategic sourcing representing tactics for buyers to leverage their buying power to ensure they attain full value. These best practices are drawn from several strategic sourcing projects carried out for leading companies in the USA over several years.

Bangkok, Thailand   Sathit Parniangtong

Acknowledgments

This book is much more than a recollection of previous experiences; it is about taking everything I learned in the past and combining it with what I know now into a story that makes sense to others. Many anecdotes came from my experience executing several consulting projects with leading companies in the USA over several years. It definitely isn't something that I could have done alone. I am extremely grateful to all people who I had contact with during my tenure at Booz, Allen & Hamilton and AT Kearney. Although I faced some difficult and challenging moments along the way, the knowledge gleaned from interacting with many great individuals has more than made up for the tough times. All of you have lifted my capabilities to a new plateau that I could never before imagine. It is difficult to know whom to acknowledge by name, because there are no clear linkages or cutoff points. However, I am extremely grateful to all who helped my professional growth.

With respect to this book, I am particularly grateful to Sasin Graduate Institute of Business Administration of Chulalongkorn University for supporting and providing a work environment that is so conducive to writing this book. I would like to express particular gratitude to those who have spent real time in advancing my writing. In particular, I would like to express my appreciation to Khun Kittiratt Na-Ranong, who paved the way for the project; my editor, Daniel Ten Kate, who was a tremendous help in making it easy for others to understand; our Sasin's Editor in Chief, Khun Wiboon Jaruwongwanich, who took the time to read and comment on the manuscript and Khun Thanaporn Julsukot, my assistant, for dealing with the complex logistics of scheduling to get all this done.

Finally, there is my family, particularly my wife, Botan, whose support and positive energy was unstoppable; and my two daughters, Beam and Beth, who provided such tremendous inspiration to writing this book and kept me in touch with reality when I begin to take things too seriously.

Contents

About the Author

Dr. Parniangtong (also known in the USA as Jack P. Chen) is President of CMBT, Strategy and Management Consulting Co. Ltd. His expertise is in competitive strategy formulation, strategy execution, and supply chain management. He also serves as Adjunct Professor at Thammasart University where he is actively addressing issues in the field of Competitive Strategy & Strategy Implementation. Over the past decade, he served as Strategy & Management Professor at Sasin Graduate Institute of Business Administration of Chulalongkorn University where he held Department Head and Administrative Positions, taught and conducted research in the areas of strategic management. He has over 20 years of consulting and work experience with international consulting firms in the USA, prior to coming back to Thailand in 2001.

He is a certified board member and serves as Chairman of the Compensation and Nomination Committee, Independent Board Member, and Member of the Audit Committee for PM Thoresen Asia Holdings Public Co. Ltd., and Patum Rice Mill and Granary Public Company Limited (Stock Exchange of Thailand-Listed companies).

He serves as strategy advisor to several SET-Listed companies in the consumer product, financial, retailing, and energy industry, and for the Royal Thai Government.

While living in the USA, where he spent almost 30 years, Dr. Sathit worked for Booz, Allen & Hamilton, and AT Kearney, where he managed consulting assignments in strategic management and operational improvements for General Motors, Inland Steel, USAir, Northwest Airline, Lucent Technology, The Department of Transportation, and The Federal Aviation Administration. He also managed oversea consulting projects in Europe, Asia and Latin America. Prior to his consulting career, he held corporate positions at American Airlines and Baxter. He also served as adjunct professor at George Washington University and University of Texas—Arlington.

Sathit has a PhD in Operations Management and Finance, Master's and Bachelor's degree in Industrial Engineering, all from the University of Wisconsin—Milwaukee.

Strategic Sourcing: Introduction

Abstract

Companies can realize significant bottom line improvement by streamlining and realigning the procurement process to reduce costs associated with the supply chain of the procured products and services. This requires management to build cooperative efforts across internal functions and seek collaborations with external business partners to weed out the inefficiencies in the supply chain. Especially on supply chain of inputs yield essential to maintaining the competitive advantage.

Keywords

Strategic sourcing • Procurement • Supply chain

Once a narrowly defined administrative function commonly referred to as "purchasing," strategic sourcing has turned into the rock upon which a company builds a competitive advantage. Leading companies realize they can reach beyond the four walls of their operations to build strategic relationships with business partners (such as suppliers and logistics service providers) and leverage these relationships to achieve the firm's strategic objectives. Adopting this new strategic approach for the procurement process requires management to elevate and expand the scope of purchasing to better align it with business objectives beyond simply focusing on minimizing the purchase price.[1] This book uses a strategic sourcing model to identify the strategic importance and financial impact of procurement activities. The model provides a framework to determine how internal procurement processes can be realigned and streamlined to support a company's goals. This strategic approach can result in lower total costs, greater revenue and improved competitiveness.

---

[1] Tim A. Minahan, Strategies for High-Performance Procurement, Supply Chain Management Review, September 2005.

Purchasing usually refers to the buying activities of employees in the finance or treasury departments. The activities are administrative in nature, designed to achieve the lowest possible purchase prices in all expenditure categories. The term "procurement" is generally broader, covering not just purchasing transactions but also materials management and ensuring that the purchased materials and services meet quality requirements. The term "strategic sourcing" takes on a different meaning. It focuses on developing channels of supply at the lowest total cost, not just the lowest purchase price. This goal requires cooperation across many other departments besides purchasing to assess the impact of procuring specific items and services from outside, especially if some of these procured materials and services are essential to maintain a company's competitive edge. For example, in the automotive industry, Original Equipment Manufacturers (OEMs), such as Toyota, Ford and GM, must consider more than simply buying a commodity like upholstery when purchasing seating since passenger comfort is a way they can differentiate their products from competitors. For this reason, Toyota Boshuku Japan spent 1.2 billion baht in 2007 to acquire local firm Thai Automotive Seating and Interior Design (TASI) after holding a 50 % stake for many years.[2]

Strategic sourcing forces a company to focus the most time and energy on strategic purchases that can provide advantages in quality, speed or cost effectiveness. In many cases, strategic sourcing plays a key role in the total cost of goods and services, which has a tremendous impact on net income and market value. In addition, strategic sourcing also helps develop long-term relationships that provide a company with multiple benefits. Both companies in the relationship can build trust and have a better understanding of how each company can mutually benefit. This often results in the deployment of best practice supply chain processes, improved customer service and company credibility as a company's product quality and service can surpass those of competitors. Costs also decline over the long run as both companies contribute to product design and jointly invest in streamlining communications and automating administrative tasks.

Strategic sourcing is a very powerful lever of (internal and external) company performance. It significantly improves company profits through reducing the supply chain cost of purchased goods, including sourcing, inventory management and transaction costs. It also helps customer relationships when a company can exceed service and quality expectations. Organizations that have implemented strategic sourcing see savings that range between 5 and 30 % of the total purchase price.[3] The savings gained from strategic sourcing vary according to the nature of goods and the degree of change proposed. Changes can include revising purchasing practices and supplier relationships, challenging product specifications and designing to radically rethink the way of doing business. Increasing the scope of change increases the size of potential benefits (see Fig. 1.1).

The magnitude of cost savings derived from this process leads to a substantially amplified result in bottom-line performance. Consider the following example (see Fig. 1.2).

---

[2] Toyota set to poursue Thai investment, Bangkok Post, August 10, 2007.

[3] Chet Hirsch and Marcos Barbalho, Toward World-Class Procurement, Supply Chain Management Review, November/December, 2001.

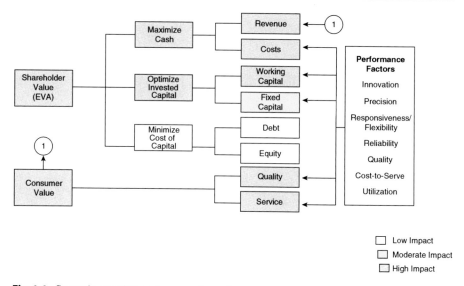

Fig. 1.1   Strategic sourcing performance impacts

Before

Revenue	$1,000
COGS Materials	700
Labor/OH	125
Gross Margin	175
Operating Expenses 75	
Net Income	$100

5% decrease in material cost ($35m)

After

Revenue	$1,000
COGS Materials	665
Labor/OH	125
Gross Margin	210
Operating Expenses	75
Net Income	$135

The alternative to achieve this increase in net income is to increase revenue by 12%*

*COGS increases by 12%

Fig. 1.2   Profit impact of reducing sourcing costs

Strategic Sourcing: Concepts, Principles and Methodology

2

Abstract

To successfully implement strategic sourcing, companies must know their most important goods and services and determine how vital they are to day-to-day operations, as well as to achieving longer-term business goals. Strategic sourcing takes on a new approach of collaboration of constituents across supply chain to better serve downstream customers that would result in enhancing longer-term profit enhancement. This chapter outlines strategic sourcing concepts, principles and methodology for executing the sourcing strategy.

Keywords

Sourcing methodology • Procurement operations • Collaborative approach • Expenditure category • Total cost of ownership

2.1 Strategic Sourcing Concepts

Strategic sourcing is the process of developing channels of supply at the *lowest total cost*, not just the lowest purchase price. It expands upon traditional purchasing activities to embrace all activities within the procurement cycle, from specification to receipt and payment of goods and services (see Fig. 2.1). Although strategic sourcing focuses primarily on reducing costs, its foundation is building longer term, win-win relationships with key suppliers to give buyers a competitive advantage.[1] The nature of the relationship underscores the success of strategic sourcing initiatives. It is critical that both buyer and supplier work together and share information to identify opportunities that will significantly increase savings over time.

---

[1] Douglas A. Smock, Robert A. Rudzki, and Stephen C. Rogers, Sourcing Strategy: The Brains Behind the Game, Supply Chain Management Review, May/June 2007.

© Springer Science+Business Media Singapore 2016

S. Parniangtong, *Supply Management*, Management for Professionals,

DOI 10.1007/978-981-10-1723-0_2

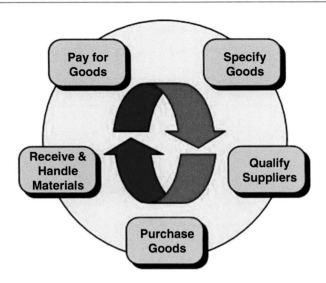

Fig. 2.1 Procurement cycle

In most companies, procurement operations are loosely coordinated. It's common to find different units within the same firm buying the same product with a different buying method that results in a different price and service level. The challenge facing a company is to obtain an optimally integrated enterprise-wide strategic procurement that allows it to leverage the purchase to achieve the most cost-effective strategic procurement of quality products at the highest level of customer service.

The transformation from traditional purchasing methods to a strategic-sourcing focus requires three fundamental philosophies that drive the strategic elements and also the infrastructure required to support the procurement process. These include:

- Focus on the total delivered value, not the purchase price
- Collaborative approach to dealing with suppliers, rather than oversight
- Focus on enhancing profitability, rather than cost savings

The above fundamental philosophies (as shown in Fig. 2.2) often result in fewer supplies. This creates economies of scale and long-standing relationships with suppliers.[2] Both the supplier and purchaser gain an advantage: they can both leverage core competencies to focus on increasing market share and improving market position.

The move from purchasing to strategic sourcing developed amid the far-reaching market changes during the 1980s. New production models based on just-in-time delivery and total quality management—as well as outsourcing, commoditization and globalization—had a profound impact on the way goods should be sourced, and

---

[2] Doug Smock, Deere Takes a Giant Leap, Purchasing, September 6, 2006.

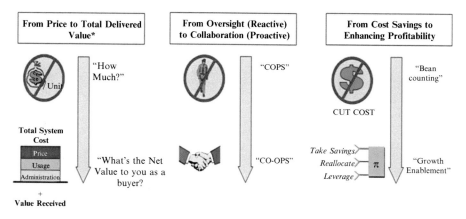

Fig. 2.2 Fundamental philosophies of strategic sourcing

on the relationship between suppliers and customers. Companies that wished to remain competitive had to shift their focus from a narrow transaction-based view of purchasing to a wider, more strategic view of how the supply chain could be configured to achieve broader corporate goals.

2.2 Strategic Sourcing Principles

A procurement strategy's overall objective is to support the ultimate goal of achieving and sustaining a company's competitive advantage. Hence, any procurement strategic initiative must be designed to support profit growth targets. This means a firm must seek ways to maximize the return on total delivered value of purchased materials, which is different from ensuring that the needed material is available at the lowest possible purchase price. The three prevailing principles in formulating and executing strategic sourcing are as follows:

Expenditure Category Strategy Formulation A product or service's strategic importance is determined by whether it has an impact on a company's core business and future competitiveness. Certain expenditure categories contribute differently to a company's success, so different strategies should be deployed depending on the goods or services that are procured. Formulating an expenditure category strategy requires a company to assess how important a resource is to the company's competitive position. However, critical resources may not be instrumental to running a company. They may be necessary, but they provide no competitive advantage in the marketplace and may have very little to do with a company's goals or mission. A good example is office supply. A business needs photocopying paper, pens and folders each day, but sourcing them is unlikely to affect a company's competitive position. On the other hand, strategic sourcing of important products will impact a

High

Complexity of the Supply Market
(External Factors)

Sourcing Management	Supply Management
A low value category that should be managed by securing supply through long-term contracts	A high value, highly complex category which should be managed through strategic partnerships
Purchasing Mgmt	Materials Management
A low category which should have minimum attention through mechanized order processing	A commodity type category which should be leveraged to maximize cost advantage

Low

Low   *Criticality of the Resource*   High
                    (internal Factors)

Criticality of Item

- Total item value
- Impact on product/service quality
- Impact on business growth
- Impact on qualitative factors (e.g., safety, environment, etc.)

Complexity of Supply

- Availability (Low)
- Number of suppliers (Few)
- Lead time risks (High)
- Substitution possibilities (No)
- Perishability/holding risks (High)

Fig. 2.3 Expenditure category strategic approach

company's position in the market. Silicon, for instance, is the key product for a microchip manufacturer as it adds value and differentiates the product from competitors. Thus, purchasing silicon is crucial to the overall product value and the company's future. If a problem occurs with silicon supply, such as poor availability or a price increase, the whole supply chain is affected, from the microchip manufacturer to the electronics manufacturer. Therefore, silicon is strategically important to a microchip manufacturer, and the purchasing process should reflect that.

In addition to understanding the strategic importance of purchasing key products, a company must also pay attention to the supply side. This will act as a guideline for specific strategies to use and the amount of time and effort that should be spent purchasing any particular item. Items with a simple supply market (high availability, large number of suppliers and plenty of substitution possibilities) are easy to purchase. Therefore, a company should devote minimal time and effort to buy them. Items with high market complexity are most likely to be high value goods or recurring needs. As the dollars spent in the long term can be significant, companies should spend the necessary time to reduce the total cost of these purchases.

A supply market's complexity is determined by how difficult it is to buy a certain item. Buying becomes difficult when a small number of suppliers are dominant and very little competition exists; buyers encounter high switching costs and lack negotiating power due to small purchase volume; suppliers have more power due to their ability to provide inputs that are important to the industry; and the supply market has high entry barriers due to, for example, major capital requirements for a startup (see Fig. 2.3). The strategic formulation for each expenditure category depends on its importance and complexity. Hence, appropriate arrangements (procurement options) must be assigned to sourcing items in each category (see Fig. 2.4 for

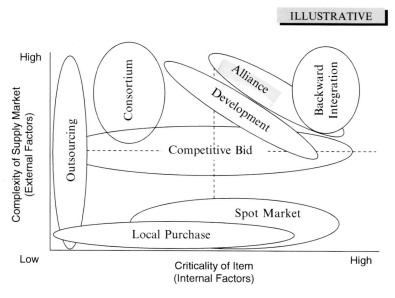

Fig. 2.4 Procurement options

arrangement of sourcing techniques). A more detailed methodology for determining the importance and complexity of an expenditure category are illustrated in later sections.

Total Supply Cost   The Strategic Sourcing concept considers the *total cost of supply*. This concept unveils the total cost incurred by the buyer when purchasing materials and services. The Total Supply Cost (TSC) is an assessment of all costs—both direct and indirect—involved with an item over the product life.[3] Most frequently, TSC is used in the purchase process to determine the most cost-effective choice. When TSC is calculated at the time a decision is made, many of the included costs are estimated because they are incurred in the future. Calculating the TSC can give buyers more detailed information to make decisions on suppliers and purchasing. It is important to know that the quoted purchase price is not the only cost involved in obtaining and using an item. An example of the TSC framework is shown in Fig. 2.5. The inclusion of all other known cost factors allows for a more complete picture to emerge. The benefits[4] of using TSC include:

- Helps focus on total value, core business, quality, yields and cycle time reduction
- Helps in understanding technical issues beyond price

---

[3] Lisa M. Ellram, Total Cost of Ownership—An Analysis Approach for Purchasing, International Journal of Physical Distribution & Logistics Management, Vol. 25 No. 8, 1995.
[4] Total Cost Modeling in Purchasing, Center for Advanced Purchasing Studies, 1994.

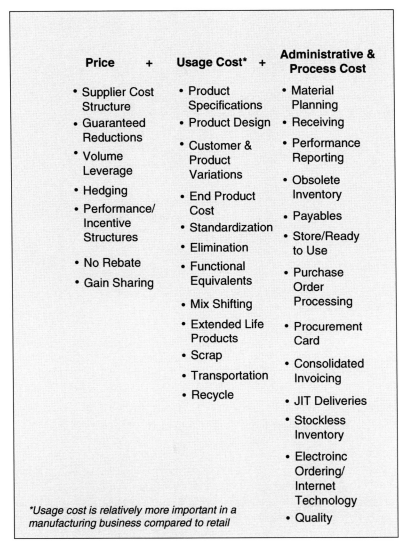

Fig. 2.5 Total supply cost

- Makes it easy to negotiate and communicate based on facts
- Drives suppliers to work on the right issues
- Pinpoints and promotes continuous supplier performance improvement
- Provides in-depth knowledge of key costs and aids in quantifying actual savings[5]
- Aids in supplier development
- Improves internal and external communications

---

[5] Zeger Degraeve and Filip Roadhooft, A Smarter Way to Buy, HBR, 2002.

- Reduces subjectivity
- Allows purchasers to determine if "something is missing"

To calculate TSC, one must first establish a framework and assumptions that will guide the work. This includes defining the needed item (or service) and determining who will use it, estimating how long the item will be in use, calculating quantities and usage rates and determining the scope of process and areas that will incur costs from using the item. Early in the process, one should define the degree to which a company is using relative vs absolute cost data. In general, three costs categories are involved in calculating the TSC. They are:

- *Incurred costs*: These are either known or can be estimated to a reasonable degree of accuracy. Incurred costs include a quoted price, transportation costs, spare parts and supplies, brokerage fees and customs duties.
- *Performance factors*: These include areas such as delivery performance, quality and requirements for service or maintenance. Performance factors are relative data. As long as the data is valid for relative comparison, it doesn't need to be an absolute cost figure.
- *Policy factors*: These encompass all issues the buying company chooses to incorporate to reflect business or social policy directives. Typically a supplier or product either meets or does not meet the policy criteria, and a firm's policymakers must establish a dollar value for it. These policies can include recycled content of materials and minority and women-owned suppliers.

For social policy factors, and other so-called "soft issues," a company must ask itself: "How much more would we be willing to pay for the privilege (or issue) being considered?" The buyer may include any soft issue in TSC as long as the company is willing to put a value on it. The buyer's value can be arbitrary, as long as it is consistent across suppliers and its relative weight makes sense to the buyer.

Several other factors must be considered in determining TSC that can affect the absolute cost comparisons between supplier A and supplier B, as well as item X and item Y. Estimates of these factors are acceptable as long as they provide a valid basis for comparison. These additional factors are:

- *Attributes of Performance*: To select suppliers that can make strategic contributions to a buyer's business, buyers need to sort out the performance variables. However, buyers should also be concerned about a supplier's respect for recycling, handling hazardous materials, safety and demographics. For example, a buyer may have a commitment to do business with minority and female-owned businesses, and we must factor these demographics into a supplier's performance.
- *Total Processing Cost*: Historically, the purchase price may have served the buyer well. But TSC takes into account many other elements that may require a more detailed methodology for calculating costs. For example, order processing costs are not the same from supplier to supplier. Importing/exporting costs and

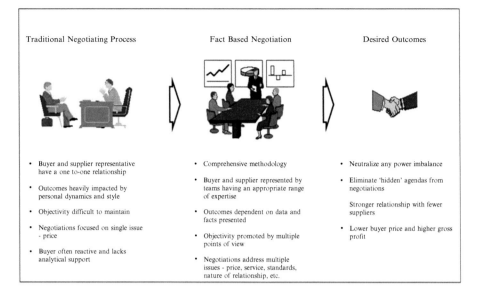

Traditional Negotiating Process	Fact Based Negotiation	Desired Outcomes
• Buyer and supplier representative have a one to-one relationship	• Comprehensive methodology	• Neutralize any power imbalance
• Outcomes heavily impacted by personal dynamics and style	• Buyer and supplier represented by teams having an appropriate range of expertise	• Eliminate 'hidden' agendas from negotiations
• Objectivity difficult to maintain	• Outcomes dependent on data and facts presented	Stronger relationship with fewer suppliers
• Negotiations focused on single issue - price	• Objectivity promoted by multiple points of view	• Lower buyer price and higher gross profit
• Buyer often reactive and lacks analytical support	• Negotiations address multiple issues - price, service, standards, nature of relationship, etc.	

Fig. 2.6 Negotiation philosophy

correction costs can also vary. Inventory costs depend on whether the supplier carries the costs or if the buyer takes ownership of the goods.

- *Weighting and Method*: After establishing the attributes of performance and cost ownership, the buyer needs to create a weighting system that converts all supplier data into a structure for making richer, better informed decisions.

The TSC can be applied to the cost of any purchase. In a manufacturing environment, it is most commonly applied to the purchase of inventory, services and Maintenance, Repair and Operating (MRO) materials.[6]

Negotiating Philosophy The successful implementation of strategic sourcing relies largely on the ability to undertake fact-based negotiations. These use a structured analytical framework based upon rigorous analysis to achieve a lower total system cost. This method, illustrated in Fig. 2.6, takes a total-cost-of-ownership (or TSC) approach to selecting suppliers rather than focusing on the purchasing price alone. This technique is suitable for high-need, high-value relationships belonging to the strategic partnership zone of the strategic sourcing model.

In contrast to a traditional negotiation process where outcomes often hinge on one-to-one personal dynamics and style, fact-based negotiation relies on comprehensive methodology. To carry out fact-based negotiation, a team of executives experienced in a range of business functions is formed. Buyers and suppliers come to the table with experts in everything from procurement, engineering and finance,

---

[6] Doug Smock, DeereTakes a Giant Leap, Purchasing, September 6, 2006.

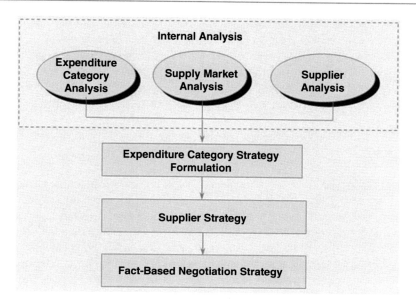

Fig. 2.7   Strategic sourcing methodology

to maintenance and research and development. The objective of the negotiation is to rely on analytical support of data and facts to address multiple issues that will develop a long and lasting relationship between the buyer and supplier. If carried out correctly, a fact-based negotiation process should produce win-win outcomes for both buyer and supplier that can ultimately lead to stronger relationships with fewer suppliers.[7]

Strategic sourcing represents a major shift from a win-lose to a win-win negotiating philosophy. It is important for both parties to negotiate with a win-win philosophy that will successfully form the basis of a long-term relationship. This approach shows that a company can lower purchasing costs without *browbeating* suppliers.

2.3   The Strategic Sourcing Methodology

Under traditional procurement methods, a purchasing department used similar methods for buying a wide variety of products and services. The chief focus was on buying items at the cheapest possible price. For example, when a company purchased large capital items, managers with technical expertise, such as engineering or information technology, often handled the decision-making and purchasing process. Managers discarded the negotiating and buying skills of purchasers in favor of so-called expertise in a product's function. In contrast, strategic sourcing recognizes

---

[7] Mark Gottfredson, Rudy Puryear, and Stephen Phillips, Strategic Sourcing—From Periphery to the Core, Harvard Business Review, February 2005.

that the skills of purchasing professionals are necessary not only for purchasing but also for decisions in other areas—product design, direction of research and development and technology uptake. All of these functions have purchasing implications and all have an impact on a company's overall profitability.[8] Rather than taking a blanket approach to securing products and services, strategic sourcing differentiates between items so that products with the highest priority command the most time and effort.

Strategic sourcing methodology consists of the following four distinct stages (see Fig. 2.7):

- Internal analysis: Analyses to understand the roles each purchased category plays in meeting strategic business objectives. If done properly, internal analyses should produce immediate short-term cost savings benefits to buyers.
- Expenditure category strategy: This stage involves determining the strategic approach, portfolio of buying options and tactics for each buying category.
- Supplier strategy: Unique category characteristics and market conditions will drive different approaches to sourcing a given expenditure category. Supplier strategy determines the overall approach for dealing with suppliers; this includes the number of suppliers, the focus of a Request for Proposal (RFP) and negotiations.
- Fact-based negotiation strategy and execution: A structured analytical framework arms the negotiating team with all facts necessary to reach the desired outcome. These stages consist of the following:
  - Negotiation strategy and case building: Defines the leverage points of buyers and suppliers and formulates strategies for countering a supplier's leverage points.
  - Supplier response and positioning: Involves anticipating supplier responses and mapping out negotiation tactics for countering a supplier's responses.
  - Negotiation planning, discussion and resolution: This process prepares a company for the actual negotiations by mapping out the logistics of engagements.
  - RFP/RFQ (Request for Quotation) preparations: RFP/RFQ provides a formatted vehicle for collecting competitive information from suppliers to aid in the negotiations.
  - Supplier selection and evaluation: This stage involves developing processes and criteria for evaluating individual suppliers. This requires a complete understanding of value received from purchasing.

Details of strategic sourcing methodology are presented in the following chapters.

---

[8] Robert B. Handfield and Samuel L. Straight, What Sourcing Channel is Right for You? Supply Chain Management Review, July/August 2003.

Strategic Sourcing: Internal Analysis

3

Abstract

In an effort to streamlining the supply chain, the company must first focus on its internal procurement process. This calls for management to perform necessary analyses to understand the strategic implications of key essential inputs and to understand the supply market of these inputs. These in-depth understandings will serve as the foundation for developing appropriate strategy for procuring the inputs deem strategic important to the company. This chapter highlights several analyses, with examples, for management to gain insight into the procured inputs.

Keywords

Supply market • Category analysis • Buying practice • Experience curve • Supplier capability • Cost driver • Order characteristic

In the first stage of strategic sourcing, the focus is on gathering information through various analyses to serve as a foundation for much of the work required in later stages.[1] The three major internal analyses are:

• Expenditure category analysis
• Supply market analysis
• Supplier analysis

---

[1] Joseph L. Cavinato, Anna E. Flynn, Ralph G. Kauffman, Supply Management Handbook, 7th Edition, McGraw-Hill 2006.

© Springer Science+Business Media Singapore 2016

S. Parniangtong, *Supply Management*, Management for Professionals,
DOI 10.1007/978-981-10-1723-0_3

3.1   Expenditure Category Analysis

This involves understanding the "as-is" situation of various current expenditure categories, which may include basic information on price, volume, product specification, current purchasing process and purchasing constraints (such as government-approved suppliers and a customer-imposed vendor list). Other analyses that proved useful include a cost breakdown analysis, supplier concentration analysis, category material substitution analysis and current purchasing contract review. Details of each of selected analyses are provided in the following section.

Category Cost Breakdown Analysis   This will provide a starting point for understanding current cost position and drivers of lower costs, which could help a company influence a product's cost. This analysis requires a cost bar waterfall that shows the costs per unit of the major representative products being purchased, indicating the major material inputs, labor, overhead and others that make up total costs (see example in Fig. 3.1). If the cost is sensitive to scale or volume, then it is helpful to draw several cost bars at low, medium and high volume levels. It is important to show cost elements that relate to the actual manufacturing process. It is also useful to put individual cost elements in two different categories. First, are the costs variable, fixed or semi-fixed? Which cost elements can be controlled by the supplier and which by the company? Second, which elements are uncontrollable? An example would be wage rates in a union plant. Cost drivers can also serve as a means to ultimately allow a company to implement measures to influence cost (see Fig. 3.2).

Category Supplier Concentration Analysis   This helps identify specific scale opportunities (other than overhead) whenever the production of a material is generally independent. Sole-sourced materials and services should be reviewed to ensure

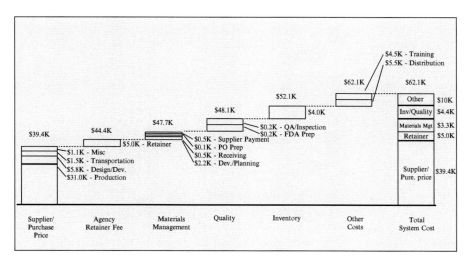

Fig. 3.1   Cost bar water fall

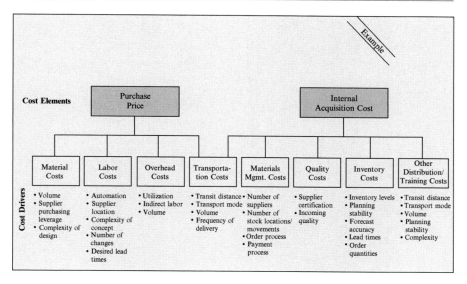

Fig. 3.2 Possible cost drivers

proper risk management and alignment with the right supplier. In short, this analysis allows a company to better understand the volume of materials being purchased from each supplier. Armed with this information, a company can then spot opportunities to consolidate its supplier base or diversify suppliers to gain leverage for bargaining. An example of this analysis is shown in Fig. 3.3.

Category Material Substitution Analysis The objective here is to determine if alternative products can fulfill a company's purchasing requirements. Substitution may occur in three areas:

- *Products that function the same but cost less*: Although this is the most obvious substitution, one must be aware of the total system cost (see next section). For example, one supplier's material may cost less but not run efficiently in the plant.
- *Standardization of materials*: A company may find opportunities to reduce the number of SKU's purchased without affecting quality or end-user requirements. A standard product will lead to fewer inventories and less obsolescence. In addition, suppliers may benefit from dedicated lines or economies of scale.
- *Product redesign*: A supplier may offer a similar product that doesn't meet the company's exact specifications but does meet quality standards and end-user requirements. For example, a cardboard box supplier to Domino's Pizza cut costs by eliminating the corners on the boxes. Using an octagonal design instead of a square not only cost less to manufacture but also resulted in a stronger box.

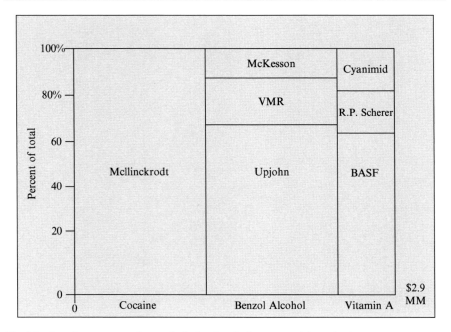

Fig. 3.3 Supplier concentration analysis for chemical raw material purchasing

Once alternative materials are identified, a company must rigorously analyze the pros and cons to determine the economic potential. Often suppliers are very willing to work with a company; executives should consult with them early and often in the process. Be sure to review the system cost impacts, as shown in Fig. 3.4.

Current Purchasing Contract Review   At the time a contract is written, its provisions are usually clear and both companies understand the implications. However, over time both the requirements and competitive environment may change. Contracts can sometimes lead to behavior that is unexpected or inconsistent with today's needs. The objective of contract review is to understand how they affect a company's purchasing behavior and competitive position; whether any constraints exist to changing practices; and what incentives—positive or negative—they provide for suppliers. When reviewing a contract, key considerations should be given to the following:

• *Terms*: Does a contract's length provide the supplier with the right economic incentive to invest in the company's business? What investment is relevant? What's the payback? How long will the technology stay relevant? For example, a contract lasting 5–7 years may induce a supplier to make a major investment in a plant, but anything less than 5 years makes a modest renovation more reasonable. What are the pros and cons of locking up supply and possibly price ceil-

1. Less expensive substitutes:				
MATERIAL (include competitor and supplier materials)	VENDOR	PRICE/ UNIT	IMPORTANT CHARAC- TERISTICS	POTENTIAL SYSTEM COST IMPACT
Item Purchased _____ Alternative A _____ Alternative B _____ Alternative C _____				

2. Standardization

ITEM PURCHASED	#SKU'S
The buying company	
Competitor A	
Competitor B	
Potential sources of SKU reduction:	_____
	_____
	_____

3. Redesign:

OPTIONS	PROS	CONS

Supplier Suggestion :

Competitor differences :

Fig. 3.4 Material substitution worksheet

ings? What does the industry and analysis suggest about future supply and demand?

- *Pricing*: What are the downstream implications of any pricing mechanism? What would happen in periods of inflation? Or if excess supply pushes down the price? Are there any price guarantees such as Most Favored Nation status? Is a guaranteed price competitive with any other pricing schemes offered to other customers? For longer-term contracts, is experience curve efficiency built into pricing mechanisms? Are any costs or savings passed through and are they monitored? How will changes in supplier volume affect the company's fixed costs?
- *Volume*: What happens if there are sudden or unexpected changes to a company's output? Can the risk of volume shifts be shared? For example, it is less risky to assign a percentage of a company's volume rather than a fixed level. What's the upside of committing volume to a supplier? For example, for suppliers with high fixed costs like can plants, maximum volume commitments (and minimal flex) should result in lower price commitments.
- *Admin*: What are the hidden costs of system-type requirements and are they necessary? What's the true cost of a scheduling procedure or audit to both the supplier and the company, and are these benefits worth the cost?
- *Changes*: What are the provisions for change? Can they handle emergencies? At what cost? Are suppliers being fairly compensated for changes?

3.2   Supplier Market Analysis

Understanding the supply market situation is a prerequisite to forming relationships with suppliers as it could give key leverage in negotiations. For example, competition among suppliers will become stronger if product demand grows slowly. This gives the buyer an opportunity to leverage its bargaining power—especially if the amount represents a significant proportion of the supplier's total production capacity. To understand the market situation, a variety of analysis frameworks are required.

Market Dynamic   Several analyses can determine growth, overall trends, market power, profitability and bargaining leverage of the supply market.

* *Supply industry size and growth analysis*: This determines industry trends and how they impact the market environment. Market size and growth provides the first insights into how suppliers view their industry and where they fit. For example, different market segments, products or regions may grow at varying rates. These trends have both cost and pricing implications, and they also may impact a supplier's desire to enter into different types of relationships. The key to understanding the market is not only its total size but also the size of the segments within it. An analysis of growth trends highlights the degree of competitiveness (and later provides an explanation for any consolidation) in an industry's environment (see Fig. 3.5).
* *Substitution analysis*: The objective of this analysis is to understand which similar products can be substituted and evaluate the impact of that trend on the marketplace. Two key issues dictate product substitution: Customer needs and system costs. If the customer perceives no difference in quality, there may be no reason to substitute. With system costs, the use of one product versus another may increase or decrease overall costs. Take steel as an example, the use of coil vs. sheet allows for faster runs and lower costs per unit. It is important to look first at what products are being replaced in the industry. This can be determined in terms of penetration or individual product growth.
* *Supply industry profitability analysis*: This aims to identify industry standards for profitability and understand the reasons for any variability or trends that impact industry pricing. Industry profitability and returns highlights an industry's competitive dimensions. It can describe a fair level of return for an industry, as well as point out cycles or any other trends. If any variations exist, then a company will need to determine their impact on pricing. This information will be important when comparing industry norms with specific suppliers (see Fig. 3.6). It will also identify value opportunities when a supplier's returns are consistently above normal levels. If a company understands what factors drive an industry's profitability, it can find leverage opportunities as a customer. It can evaluate profitability, return on sales, return on assets and return on equity.
* *Market fragmentation/consolidation analysis*: An industry's degree of fragmentation creates more sophisticated relationships and determines proper pricing.

	Data
1. Total Market Size — In dollars / In units	_____ / _____
2. Size of Market Segments — Defined by: Product Types	
	Defined by: Customer Segments	
	Defined by: Region (if relevant)	
3. Market Growth Rates — Total Market (units) Region (if relevant) Historically / Future forecast	
	Total Market (constant $) Region (if relevant) Historically / Future forecast	
4. Segment Growth Rates — ____ ___Segment growth rate_ Historically / Future forecast	
	____ __Segment growth rate_ Historically / Future forecast	

Fig. 3.5 Supply industry market size and growth worksheet

Has the industry consolidated? What are future trends? In a consolidating industry, large customers must ensure they are aligned with the winners. Evaluating
the likelihood of consolidation requires thorough knowledge of an industry's
barriers to entry. Industries with high barriers are more likely to consolidate than
those in which companies can enter with ease.

	Current Year	History												
	19__	19__	19__	19__	19__	19__	19__	19__	19__	19__	19__	19__	19__
Operating Profit													
• Total sales													
• Total assets													
• Equity													
• Oper. ROS													
• Oper. ROA													
• Oper. ROE													

Fig. 3.6 Industry profitability returns matrix worksheet

- *Supply industry technology analysis*: This determines what role technology plays in an industry's competitive dynamics and the accessibility of that technology to all players. As a purchaser of a particular product, a company must ask these questions about the technology: Will it improve product quality? Does it decrease the price per unit? Technology leadership may be linked to cost leadership. It may be valuable for a company to link up with the technology leader, and design a strategy to capture or share the cost savings. This analysis may involve evaluating the role of technology in an industry, tracing its evolution and its impact on quality and cost, as well as determining the accessibility of key technologies and the role of individual companies in R&D (see Fig. 3.7).

Suppliers/Customer Buying Practices Comparing a customer's relative strengths with a supplier's relative strengths may explain the different types of relationships and the power balances in them. Two analyses in particular are worth exploring to understand the supply industry:

- *Industry customer analysis*: This analysis determines the role the customer plays in the industry's competitive environment. Relative customer leverage may help influence underlying economic conditions and marketplace complexity. Exploring the customer market will explain details about an industry's competitive dynamics. Do one or two large customers dominate an industry or specific market segments? A company may gain some additional leverage if the supplier faces a high cost of reconfiguring a product to meet another customer's specifications (see Fig. 3.8).

			Data
	Industry Research & Development	Current ($ spent)	$_____
		Historic (if relevant) 199_ 19__ 19__ 19__ 19__	$_____ $_____ $_____ $_____ $_____
1. Technology's Role in an Industry	Industry Research & Development	Number of Patents (if relevant) 199_ 19__ 19__ 19__ 19__	$_____ $_____ $_____ $_____ $_____
	Impact on Cost		
	Impact on Quality		

	Technology	Description	Relevant Company/Org.	Introduction	Impact
2. Recent and Historic Developments					

3. Accessibility of Technology	

Fig. 3.7 Supply industry technology worksheet

1. Market Size (from market size/growth section)	
2. Size of Market Segments (from market size/growth section)	

	Customer	Total Market ($ or units)	By Segment (if relevant) $ or Units)		
3. Customers					
	Others				

Fig. 3.8 Supply industry customer worksheet

- *Buying practice analysis*: To analyze purchasing patterns within an industry, look for demand trends on a weekly or monthly basis. This could be compared to segment purchasing to determine if any peculiarities or differences exist between the two. Buying patterns may indicate seasonal variations in price and may significantly impact capacity constraints within an industry. At this level of anal-

		Jan	Feb	Mar	Apr	May	Jun	Jul	Aug	Sep	Oct	Nov	Dec
1. Seasonal Variations	• Market Sales ($ or units)												
	• Segment Sales ($ or units)												
	• Price Variations ($ or units)												
2. Regional Buying Patterns (if relevant)	(a) Does demand different for different regions throughout the year? (yes or no) If yes, do the above variations chart by region?	_____ _____											
3. Other Variations (contact associations, industry experts for other possible patterns)	(a) Different order sizes (b) Variability – same product from differing SKU (measure ACME Co. company variations if industry variations are not measurable)	_____ _____ – _____ _____ –											

Fig. 3.9 Supply industry buying practices worksheet

ysis, however, it is important to understand how much the variation is driven by customer purchase patterns versus fundamental supply issues (see Fig. 3.9).

Industry Economic/Pricing   An understanding of price and cost drivers within an industry allows buyers to compare the price curve with the supplier's cost curve. The differences may present an opportunity to further negotiate for price concessions or increase delivery values for products. Two analysis frameworks are commonly used:

- *Experience curve*: Marketplace dynamics drive price. Changes in the supply/ demand balance, competition and consumer value perception relative to substitution products all cause real prices to fall over time. Experience curves measure the relationship between the increase in accumulated experience and the drop in the unit price (or cost). Thus, on a log-log scale, prices will fall by x% every time the accumulated volume doubles. Experience curves illustrate the decline in real prices over time at a fairly constant rate under the assumption that competitive and supply/demand conditions are normal. If prices do not decline at the same time rate, the supplier may build a "price umbrella." This may provide the customer with an opportunity to "break" the umbrella and cause prices to continue declining steadily (see Fig. 3.10).
- *Industry cost bar analysis*: The objective is to understand roughly what factors play a key role in driving costs. Determining an industry's cost structure and the underlying cost drivers is vital to understanding particular elements of an industry's economics and may provide key input into areas to focus supply chain effi-

ciencies. Precision will not be as valuable as relative importance. Thus, if cost data is not readily available, conversations with industry associations and experts may be sufficient. These conversations may also suggest some specific cost drivers (see Fig. 3.11).

1. Estimation of Accumulated Volume (x-axis) – Only if statistics are not available from Historical Statistical Abstract						$2/3 \times \dfrac{\text{(volume in earliest year)}}{\text{(CAGR* from earliest to latest year)}}$							
2.	Current Year					History							
	19__	19__	19__	19__	19__	19__	19__	19__	19__	19__	19__	19__	19__
• Constant Prices													
• Accumulated volume (amt. from above plus given year's volume)													
• Ln (price)													
• Ln (accum. volume)													
3. Other Segments (if relevant); fill out chart as above													

* * - Compound Annual Growth Rate

Fig. 3.10   Supply industry experience curve worksheet

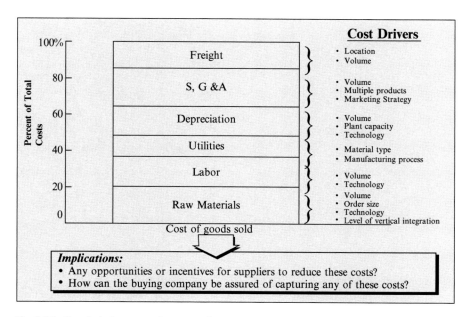

Fig. 3.11   Supply industry cost bar example

3.3   Supplier Analysis

For expenditure categories, the search for viable suppliers is a continuous process as new suppliers will always enter a profitable market. Information about individual suppliers serves as a cornerstone for deploying the most appropriate sourcing strategy and negotiation tactics.[2] Before a company conducts a detailed analysis on individual suppliers, the number of suppliers should be systematically screened from all possible suppliers (see Fig. 3.12). This means a firm should cast a wide net to include current, alternative and non-traditional suppliers to capture all viable suppliers for detailed analysis. Current suppliers are those with established relationships and baseline expenditures. Alternative suppliers are often the competitors of current suppliers that offer similar goods and services. Non-traditional suppliers are candidates with a relatively untested capability to supply the needed products. The number of suppliers varies according to the expenditure category.

To screen suppliers, the first step is to send a request for information (RFI) to possible suppliers so a company can develop a short list. The RFI may include general information about the company, product lines, service levels, capability, quality control and other requirements deemed appropriate. In addition to information requested through an RFI, a company needs details on supplier profitability. This is used to estimate supplier cost structure and annual cost changes by product line, as well as to determine the supplier's financial capability and stability. This information is collected from public information sources like

Fig. 3.12 Supplier
analysis list development

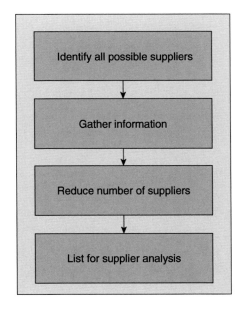

---

[2] Robert Monczka, Robert Trent, and Robert Handfield, Purchasing and Supply Chain Management, 3rd edition, Thomson, South-western, 2005.

Supplier Scorecard			
Supplier Name:			
Criteria	Score	Weighting	Weighted Score
Capability	90	10%	9
Time	80	10%	8
Quality	70	20%	14
Service	100	10%	10
Cost	90	30%	27
Lead Time	90	20%	18

Fig. 3.13 Supplier scorecard for shortlisting

financial statements, industry publications, public comments, industry contacts and corporate reports.

After reviewing the available information, a company should cut down the list of suppliers to a reasonable number using "go no-go" criteria. These include whether a supplier is too small, doesn't have enough capacity, has insufficient distribution coverage, has a poor track record with the buyer, has a poor market image or has an unsophisticated quality control program. If necessary, the criteria should be selected and weighted to further reduce the number of suppliers (see Fig. 3.13). The result will be a list for a detailed supplier analysis.

An in-depth analysis of each supplier is necessary for a company to determine their strengths and weaknesses within the context of the buyer bargaining position. Individual suppliers can be analyzed in three ways: capability, cost and profitability:

Supplier Capability Supplier capability is one of the most important factors that determine how a supplier will behave during the negotiation process. Understanding a supplier's capability will serve as the basis for formulating negotiation tactics that could lead to a win-win outcome. To better understand a supplier's capacity, a company should perform the following analyses:

- A supplier size and market share analysis determines a supplier's market presence. A company must first know the size of each supplier within the industry. Suppliers that need to grow and gain market share will value the company's business more than other suppliers. Some suppliers may dominate only one segment of the market and wish to expand into other segments if given the opportunity. In addition, in industries where economies of scale are important, the market

leader will have lower costs than other suppliers. Buyers can take advantage of
this in price negotiations.

• When a supplier's strategic direction is aligned with a company's purchasing
  needs, it increases the opportunity for reaching a win-win outcome. Knowing a
  supplier's strategy helps a company predict what a relationship or partnership
  may look like. Ideally, the supplier's strategic outlook should complement the
  company's purchasing strategic outlook. A true mutual competitive advantage
  can be created when the company works with suppliers whose strategic
  imperatives are best met by serving the company rather than another customer.
  For example, when purchasing cans, one company may provide volume commitments out of individual plant locations that no other customer can match.
  However, the company is not the largest commercial can customer in the country. Therefore, the company will create more value for a can maker who wants to
  dominate individual regions than for one with a strategy to win national contracts
  (see examples in Figs. 3.14 and 3.15).

• A company must know the importance of its business to a supplier so it understands its place and potential within the supplier's customer portfolio. The company's relative importance to the supplier can determine how much leverage the
  company has in negotiations. A supplier that is increasingly dependent on the
  company's business should be more responsive to its buying demands than other
  suppliers. Furthermore, if scale is vital to a supplier's cost position, it will be
  cheaper for it to serve large customers than smaller clients. These advantages
  must be weighed against the risk of relying too heavily on only one supplier,
  which include unexpected business interruptions and the lack of competitive bidding or market pressure. A buyer may calculate what percentage of a supplier's
  business it accounts for by looking at sales, unit volume or profit. Is the buying

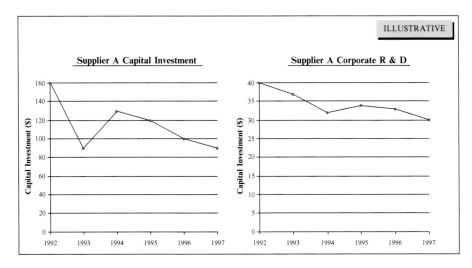

Fig. 3.14 Supplier strategy: capital investment

company the supplier's largest customer? Or is the largest customer in a supplier's market segment? (See Fig. 3.16.)
- The specific supplier technology analysis determines a supplier's short-term and long-term competitiveness. If technology leadership is essential to a company's costs or quality standards, then it should identify opportunities to work with the technology leaders. The purchasing approach (such as alliance, backward inte-

---

"During 1996 and 1995, the focus of the company's operations has been to improve the performance and increase the value of the company's core businesses. Businesses which do not fit the long-term objectives of the company or which do not provide satisfactory returns on the company's investment have been sold."

- Owens-Illinois Annual Report

"I don't mind licensing our technology because technology agreements push our R&D people to decrease our costs further, which they've always been able to do."

- Joe Lemieux, CEO

"Licensing agreements are very profitable for us. They are an excellent way to leverage our technology after we've used it."

- Dan Whiting, VP sales

Fig. 3.15 Supplier strategy: example — glass products

	Current Year	History					
	19	19	19	19	19	19	19
Total supplier sales	___	___	___	___	___	___	___
Sales to the buyer	___	___	___	___	___	___	___
The buyer's business as % total sales	___	___	___	___	___	___	___
Average growth							
— Total sales 1992-1997	___						
— Buyer's sales 1992-1997	___						
Other major customers - - Sales							
___	___	___	___	___	___	___	___
___	___	___	___	___	___	___	___
___	___	___	___	___	___	___	___
___	___	___	___	___	___	___	___

Fig. 3.16 Importance of the Buyer's business worksheet

gration or supplier development) must help the supplier make ongoing investments in the latest technology so both sides can share the savings. The importance of technology varies by industry. Advances and improvements occur over different time horizons. Analyzing specific supplier technology requires the buying company to identify the range of technologies used in an industry. A company must assess each supplier's capabilities and then determine the approximate cost and quality benefits associated with the latest technology, as well as the penalty incurred from using old technology. Then the company can compare the benefits of technology to the required investment to understand which suppliers are likely to make those investments.

- To assist in supplier selection, a company should conduct a supplier quality and service analysis. Quality and service levels are not easy to quantify. Most of the analysis is based on ranking or perception. But for issues such as reliability and turnaround time, suppliers should be ranked relative to one another. In these cases, it is important to decide which issues are the most important to both the purchasing department and also the user (the plant). A supplier may have a reputation for providing excellent new products, but the plant may be more interested in flexibility (see Figs. 3.17 and 3.18).

Supplier Cost Analysis Understanding a supplier's cost structure is useful to a buyer because it can collaborate with the supplier to bring down costs and share the savings. In addition, knowing which supplier is the most cost competitive (with the record of bringing down costs the fastest), the buyer can expect to benefit from lower purchasing prices. Finally, every manufacturing operation has an optimal eco-

Factor	Importance Ranking	Supplier Performance			
		A	B	C	D
1. Turnaround on last minute orders					
2. Reliability of deliveries					
3. Reject rate per 000 at incoming inspection					
4. Reject rate at plant (during operations)					
5. Collaboration on new product development					
6. Flexibility of volume changes					
7. Accuracy of order fills					
8. Quality and timeliness of response					
9. Other _____					
Comments:					

Fig. 3.17 Supplier quality and service worksheet

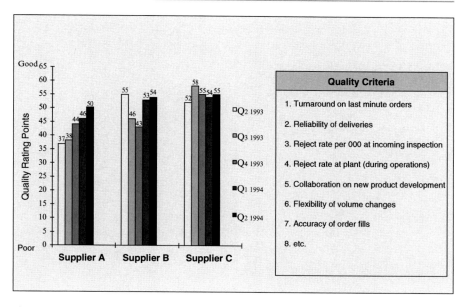

Fig. 3.18 Supplier quality and service example: paint supplier quality rating

nomic run (the optimal amount of quantity produced in a production run). A buyer who can determine the optimal quantity can take advantage of this by matching the purchased quantity with the supplier's optimal economic run. The sections below provide examples of selected supplier cost analyses.

- The supplier cost drivers analysis helps identify a supplier's costs. This analysis is most useful when the buyer has a choice of suppliers and/or can collaborate with suppliers to bring costs down. It is relevant in a competitive bidding situation where price—not cost—is the main issue. The process begins by selecting costs that can be cut easily, usually those that are the largest and most controllable. Identify what activity or condition accounts for the difference in cost. For example, in raw materials the key factor might be volume purchase, whereas in labor, the key factor might be throughput. In general, a company should work with suppliers that are set up to offer lower costs. If a supplier is well suited for long runs and the company needs short runs and maximum flexibility, the low-cost supplier will not be suitable. The company should then work with suppliers to find opportunities to lower costs in a way in which both sides can share the savings. Figure 3.19 illustrates supplier cost elements and cost drivers that can be used for the buying company and supplier to work together to bring down costs.
- The supplier experience curve analysis can be conducted to determine the supplier's competitiveness. The basic principle behind the experience curve is that costs to provide a given product should decline as the supplier becomes more experienced providing that product. Cost is expressed in constant dollars (adjusted for inflation) and placed on the Y axis using a logarithmic scale. Accumulated experience is placed on the X axis also using a logarithmic scale.

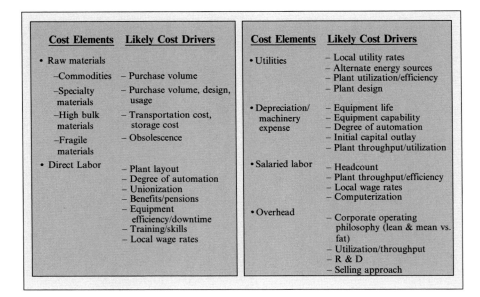

Fig. 3.19 Supplier cost material drivers checklist

Theoretically, suppliers will have different cost experience curves with different slopes. Points of inflection and "kinks" in the curve suggest a technology breakthrough, material substitution or major manufacturing process change. For every doubling of accumulated experience, costs decline by 1 minus the slope. For example, if XYZ Company has an 80 % cost experience curve and it doubles its accumulated experience between 1993 and 1997, then costs in 1997 will be (1–0.80), or 20 % lower than in 1993. It is important to remember that suppliers have not only different slopes but different amounts of accumulated experience. If all suppliers had the same slope, then the supplier with the most experience would have the lowest cost. A supplier that manages to decrease its costs faster than others (given the same rate of experience accumulation) should be able to pass the savings on to the buying company in the form of lower prices. In addition, the experience curve is useful for predicting a supplier's future profitability. When a supplier's industry faces intense competition, the price experience curve may drop sharply. If the supplier has not managed its costs over the years, its cost experience may actually be flatter than the price experience curve. In this situation, the supplier must make radical changes in its cost structure or else go out of business (see Fig. 3.20).

- Cost comparisons can also be used to assess current expenditures. Several methods can be used to perform cost comparisons, including comparing current price to historical prices (see Fig. 3.21 for details). If the buyer purchases several items (or a basket of similar items), a supplier pricing index can also be established to track supplier prices (see Fig. 3.22). After obtaining a supplier price index, the

<u>**Cost**</u>

	Costs/Unit Current $	Deflator		Costs/Unit ÷ Deflator	=	Costs/Unit In 1990 $
Current Year: 19__						
History 19__						
19__						
19__						
19__						
19__						

Accumulated Experience

	Prior Experience*		Accumulated Experience
Current Year: 19__		- - - →	
History 19__			
19__			
19__			
19__			
19__			

$$*\text{Prior experience} = \frac{2}{3} \times \frac{(\text{Volume earliest year available})}{(\text{Compound annual growth rate from earliest to latest year})}$$

Fig. 3.20 Supplier experience curve worksheet

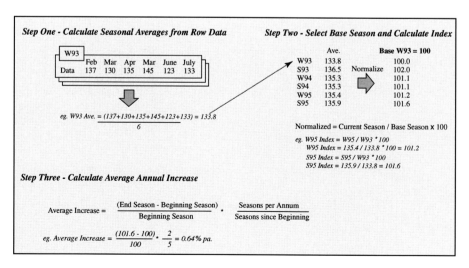

Fig. 3.21 Supplier price index example

buyer should compare this against the acceptable industry price movement and request the savings from the difference (see Figs. 3.23 and 3.24).

- A buyer can benefit from understanding the particular cost drivers that lead to low costs in scale operations. Every manufacturing technology has some sort of scale curve, meaning that high volumes cost less per unit than small volumes. However, the appropriate unit of scale varies according to product and technology. Generally, scale effects occur when significant fixed costs are linked to the

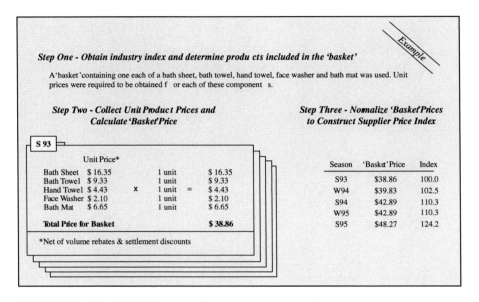

Fig. 3.22 Supplier pricing index example

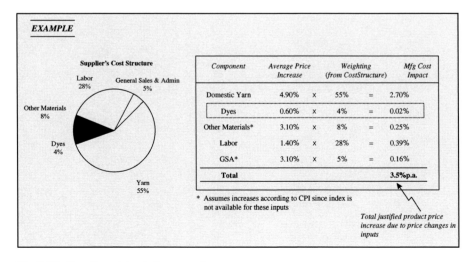

Fig. 3.23 Supplier pricing index example

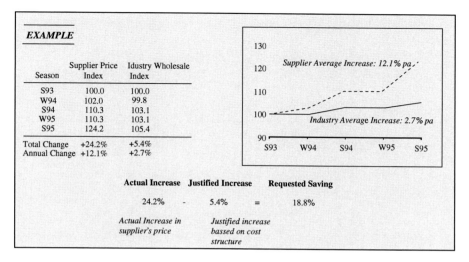

Fig. 3.24 Supplier and industry pricing index comparison example

process. For example, the major fixed cost in printing labels is the changeover and setup of the printing press. Long runs of a single label are much more economical than short runs. In most cases, the buyer should strive to purchase in a form and quantity that takes advantage of the scale curve. This means buying enough to get the lower costs, but not buying more than is needed once the scale effects taper off. However, transportation scale must be taken into account as well.

Supplier Profitability Analysis Understanding a supplier's financial condition allows a buyer to determine if price reductions are possible and if the supplier can finance investments in new technology. Specific supplier profitability analyses are presented below:

- A ratio analysis can be used to understand a supplier's financial strengths and weaknesses. This best serves as a preliminary check on a supplier's profitability, financial liquidity and leverage, fixed asset management and shareholder returns. It can identify whether a price reduction possibility exists with a particular supplier. The analysis is also important for understanding whether a supplier faces financial troubles, and how serious the problems are (see Figs. 3.25, 3.26 and 3.27 for specific ratios).
- It's crucial for a buyer to know the profit a supplier earns from each transaction to avoid paying a price premium. Ideally, the buying company's goal would look to gain a pricing advantage while allowing the supplier to realize normal or above-normal profits over the long term. It is important for the supplier to achieve hurdle rate returns. Buyers want to avoid paying a price premium that the supplier can use to buy (subsidize) other businesses.

Ratio	Formula	Significance
Return on sales		
• Gross profit margin	• (Sales - cost of goods sold) ÷ sales	• Measure of profitability before S,G &A
• Operating profit margin	• Profit before tax ÷ sales	• Measure of operating profitability
• Return on sales	• Net income ÷ sales	• Measure of bottom line company profitability
Return on investment		
• Return on total assets	• Net income + (interest expense × [1-tax rate]) ÷ average total assets	• Measure of how well assets have been employed by management
• Return on common stock holders' equity	• (Net income - preferred dividends) ÷ average common stockholders' equity	• When compared to the return on total assets, measures the extent to which leverage is being employed for or against the common stockholders
Risk: Debt structure		
• Times interest earned	• Earning before interest expense and income taxes ÷ interest expense	• Measure of the likelihood that creditors will continue to receive their interest payments
• Dept-to-equity ratio	• Total liabilities ÷ stockholders' equity	• Measure of the amount of assets being provided by creditors for each dollar of assets being provided by the stockholders

Fig. 3.25 Supplier ratio summary

Ratio	Formula	Significance
Liquidity: Ability to meet current obligations		
• Working captial	• Current assets – current liabilities	• Represents assets financed from short-term sources that do not require near-term repayment
• Current ratio	• Current assets ÷ current liabilities	• Text of short-term debt paying ability
• Acid test ratio	• (Cash + Marketable securities + current receivable) ÷ current liabilities	• Text of short-term debt paying ability with out having to rely on inventory
• Accounts receivable turnovers	• Sales on account ÷ average accounts receivable balance	• Text of quality of accounts receivable
• Average collection period (days receivables)	• 365 ÷ accounts receivable turnover	• Text of quality of accounts receivable in terms of average age in days
• Accounts payable turnover	• Purchases on account ÷ average accounts payable balance	• Measure of how manytimes the accounts payable balance is paid
• Average payable period (days Payable)	• 365 ÷ accounts payable turnover	• Days that it takes to payan accounts payable balance
• Inventory turnover	• Cost of goods sold ÷ average inventory balance	• Measure of how many times a company's inventory has been sold during the year
• Days required to sell the inventory (average sale period)	• 365 ÷ inventoryturnover	• Measure of the number of days required to sell the inventory one time

Fig. 3.26 Supplier ratio summary cont'd

Ratio	Formula	Significance
Shareholders perspective- "Pershare" ratio		
• Earnings pershare (of common stock)	• Net income less preferred dividends ÷ number of common shares outstanding	• Tends to have an effrect on the market price per share ,as reflected in the price-earnings ratio
• Fully diluted earnings per share	• Net income less preferred dividends ÷ (number of common shares + common stock equivalent of convertible securities)	• Shows the protential effect on earnings per share of converting convertible securities into common stock
• Price earnings ratio	• Current market price pershare ÷ earnings pershare	• An index of whether a stock is a relatively cheap or relatively expensive
• Dividends payout ratio	• Dividends pershare ÷ earnings pershare	• An index of whether a company pays out most of its earning in dividends or reinvests the earnings internally
• Dividends yield ratio	• Dividends pershare ÷ market price per share	• Shows the dividend return being provided by a stock,which can be compared to the return being provided by other stocks
• Book value per share	• Total Net-worth ÷ number of common shares	• Measures the amount which would be distributed to each share of common stock if assets were liquidated at their balance sheet amounts. (Based entirely on historical costs)

Fig. 3.27 Supplier ratio summary cont'd

A company must determine if suppliers earn more profit from its business than from other firms. A supplier may be reluctant to provide cost data in the form of cost per unit. Usually, all the buying company will know about its price. If the supplier gives the buying company a discount to its competitors, it may appear that the buying company's business is actually less profitable to the supplier. However, the supplier's profitability is determined by both price and cost. For some products, the company's purchases may be significantly cheaper to produce than another firm's purchases. Some cost drivers that can make a buying company's business more profitable include: large volumes that allow for economies of scale; easier designs that can be run faster; a previous investment in a plant and equipment; and a predictable volume. Identifying these factors requires the buying company to determine areas where its business gives the supplier a cost advantage compared to other customers.

In some cases, an entire manufacturing line or plant may be devoted to a company's business, and the cost data may be provided. In that case, a buyer can make a rough estimate of its costs by dividing the total cost of the line or plant by the purchased volume.

• A supplier cash flow analysis determines a supplier's health. The cash flow will reveal whether or not a supplier can afford necessary investments, and whether it has sufficient funds to invest in new technology. In addition, a supplier with excessive cash flow can cut prices for the buying company. A supplier in financial distress may represent a poor risk for the buyer. Two types of cash flow analyses can be conducted: Operating cash flow and financial cash flow. Cash flow equals the sum of operating cash flow plus financial cash flow. Operating cash flow measures the ability of a supplier's recurring operations to generate cash. As a formula, it looks like this: Operating profit + non-cash expenses included in operating profit − capital expenditures − increases in non-cash operating working capital accounts − taxes paid. Financial cash flow captures all the non-operating cash changes experienced during the year and provides information on how a company funds its operations. It includes debt-related transactions (issuing or paying off debt), equity-related transactions (issuing or purchasing the company's stock), long-term asset and liability transactions (buying or selling non-operating items) and one-time events (like asset sales). Figure 3.28 presents a cash flow analysis of an individual supplier for comparison purposes.

Figure 3.29 shows a work sheet summarized supplier analysis that includes a supplier's capability, costs and profitability.

	Supplier A	Supplier B	Supplier C
Operating Cash Flows			
+ Pre-tax operating profit			
+ Non-cash expense			
- Increase in working capital			
- Taxes paid			
Net operating cash flow			
Financial Cash Flows			
+ Increase debt			
- Debt retired			
+ Equity issued			
- Equity repurchases			
+ Liquidation of non-operating investments			
- Investments in non-operating assets			
+ / - One time events			
Net financial cash flow			
Net corporate cash flow			

Fig. 3.28 Supplier cash flow worksheet

	Key Insight		
Analysis	Supplier A	Supplier B	Supplier C
Key Players & Capabilities:			
- Size and Market Share			
- Strategy			
- Importance of Buyer's Business			
- Technology			
- Quality and Service			
Costs:			
- Cost Bar			
- Cost Experience Curve			
- Cost Drivers			
- Units of Scale			
- Relative Cost Position			
Profitability:			
- Ratio Analysis			
- Profitability of Buyer's Business			
- Cash Flow			

Fig. 3.29   Summary: supplier analysis worksheet

Internal Analysis Case Study

As much as the analyses presented above can help a buying company formulate its procurement strategy and negotiation tactics, they can also lead to short-term benefits. Take the example of a St. Louis-based diversified global manufacturer that combines technology and engineering to provide innovative solutions to customers. The company is ranked number two in the electronics industry with thousands of patents in industrial automation, climate control technologies and the tool business. With more than 270 manufacturing locations, of which about 200 are located outside the USA, the company has recently focused its efforts on providing turnkey solutions and after-sale service for customers. For example, the company provides around-the-clock support for uninterrupted power supply and protects food safety with remote monitoring of supermarket refrigeration equipment and compressor rooms.

The company has entered new geographic markets, developed new products, created new partnerships and delivered integrated solutions and systems that address some of the most important challenges facing its customers. In developing regions, new telecommunications infrastructure that facilitates Internet access has increased the demand for uninterrupted power, plant

(continued)

automation and telecommunication systems. These growth initiatives are supported by the company's long-term commitment to maintain operational excellence and deliver complete customer satisfaction. This involves identifying operational improvements, cost efficiencies and asset utilization.

The company recognizes that material procurement and lean manufacturing initiatives will enable it to provide customers with a faster response time and higher quality at competitive prices.

Although the company manufactures many highly technical components, its vendors around the world procure a vast majority of parts. The company has recently launched e-business strategies in a range of business and sales operations to achieve cost savings, improve productivity and better serve customer needs. With more than one million purchased stock-keeping units (SKUs), the company participates in Internet auctions to lower procurement costs and increase efficiency. In addition, the company has developed a proprietary network that provides key distributors with real-time information on parts availability and delivery. This new point-to-point system gained acceptance from distributors due to its speed (a 1-to-2 s response time) and accuracy.

In an effort to further improve its operational effectiveness, the company launched a study to streamline the procurement process while maintaining excellent customer service. Initially, the company singled out one of its largest procurement categories—the fuse category. Three analyses were performed in parallel to identify opportunities for improving end-to-end (vendor to customer) operational improvements. These included:

Category performance analysis: This identifies opportunities for improving costs through SKU rationalization and substitution. A series of analyses are performed to support the analysis framework to determine how individual SKUs contribute to revenue and profit as shown in Figs. 3.A, 3.B, 3.C, and 3.D.

Customer analysis: This aims to find areas in which the company can improve its operations while still keeping customers happy. Figure 3.E indicates that the majority of SKUs are sold infrequently and in low volume. In addition, the demand for the majority of these fuses occurs only in a small number of branches (see Fig. 3.F). This represents an opportunity for the company to centralize the fuses at only a few branches to improve inventory turnover, which may result in longer delivery times as the fuses are shipped from further away (see Fig. 3.G). However, upon reviewing customer buying value (as shown in Fig. 3.H), availability is relatively less important than other factors. Hence, a centralized inventory with an improved delivery schedule represents promising opportunities for improvement. Figure 3.I indicates that average monthly demand is significantly less than

(continued)

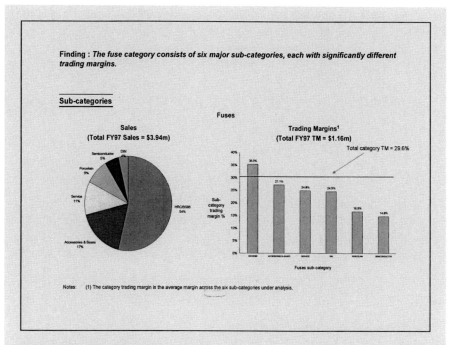

Fig. 3.A   Category performance analysis

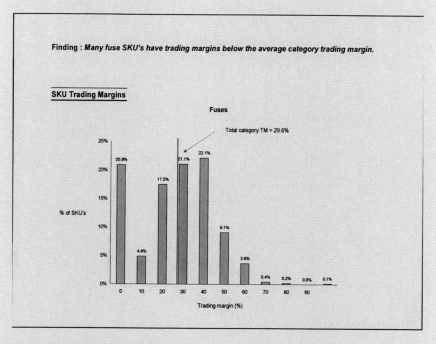

Fig. 3.B   Category performance analysis

(continued)

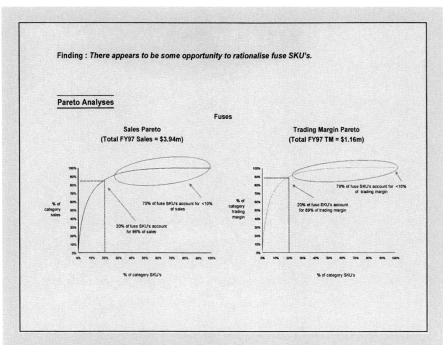

Fig. 3.C   Category performance analysis

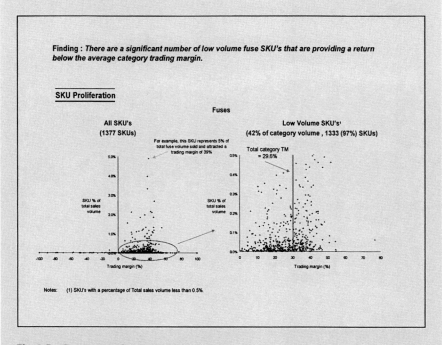

Fig. 3.D   Category performance analysis

(continued)

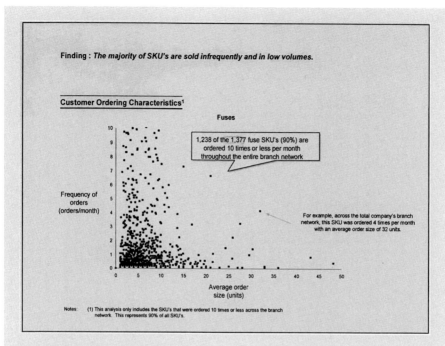

Fig. 3.E   Category performance analysis

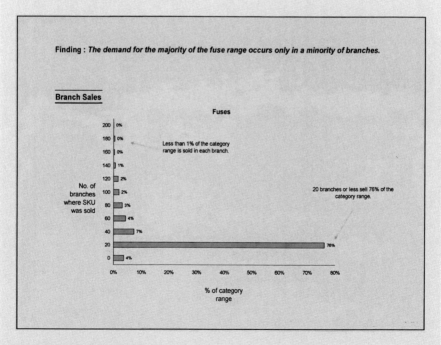

Fig. 3.F   Category performance analysis

(continued)

Finding : *There is some opportunity to remove slow moving stock and cost from the branches by distributing fuses through the company distribution centre.*

Rationalisation Opportunities

Fuses	Product Rationalisation Candidates[1]			Obsolete Candidates[2]
	IHC>TM (where IHC=10%)	IHC>TM (where IHC=20%)	TM <15%, >0%	
No. of SKU's	212	322	168	198
% of Total	15.4	23.4	12.2	14.4
Branch stock ($)	0.207	0.421	0.076	0.019
Warehouse stock($m)	0	0	0	0
Total stock on hand ($m)	0.207	0.421	0.076	0.019
Trading margin ($m)	0.01	0.052	0.037	0

Notes: (1) Rationalisation candidates have been determined by calculating the inventory holding cost for each SKU, and comparing it to the trading margin earned on theSKU. The inventory holding cost has been adjusted by the stock turn. Where the inventory holding cost exceeds the trading margin the SKU has been identified as a candidate for rationalisation.
(2) SKU's with zero sales for FY97 have been assumed to be obsolete candidates.

Fig. 3.G Category performance analysis

Category:	Fuses	Key Customers
Sub category:	HRC / BS88, DIN, Semiconductor	Purchases are once off and very infrequent. Project sales are also considered as OEM purchases.
Customer segment:	Projects	

Buyer Value	Definition of Buyer Value	Importance of Buyer Value					Other Service Requirements (eg. make to order, cut lengths, multiple delivery sites)
		Very Impt.				Not Impt.	
Price	Customer expects consistent and best prices compared with competitors	①1	2	3	4	5	
Quality	Customer expects reliable, durable and undamaged product	1	②2	3	4	5	
Service	Customer expects the product to be delivered direct to site	①1	2	3	4	5	
Availability	Customer expects the product to be available immediately	1	2	③3	4	5	Delivery schedules may be given.
Brand loyalty	Customer will look for and only purchase well known brands	1	2	③3	4	5	
Product variety	Customer expects - a wide selection of brands - a wide selection of products	1 1	2 2	3 3	④4 ④4	5 5	
Product and technical knowledge	Customer values good technical and product knowledge	1	2	3	④4	5	

Fig. 3.H Category performance analysis

(continued)

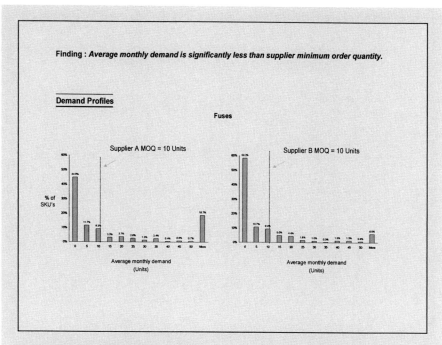

Fig. 3.I Category performance analysis

the supplier's minimum order quantity (MOQ). Therefore, removing MOQ or sell-through should be the focus of supplier negotiations.

Supplier analysis: This provides a "snapshot" of a supplier's operations and performance, and identifies its strengths and weaknesses from a buyer's perspective. Conducting a supplier analysis should be done together with customer demand for each product and corresponding trading margins in order to spot potential opportunities for supplier consolidation. This will provide a buyer with volume leverage for a better service and price. As shown in Fig. 3.J, four of the six major subcategories are now supplied by three or more suppliers. A further analysis, as shown in Fig. 3.K, indicated that the trading margins and purchase amounts within each subcategory differ significantly. This analysis allows a buyer to initially pinpoint selected suppliers for consolidating volume. However, trading margins alone are not sufficient. Buyers must also consider other supplier capabilities for the consolidated volume (see Fig. 3.L for an analysis on supplier strengths and weaknesses). The other objective for conducting a supplier analysis is to identify alternative suppliers for a category. A logical approach for determining the need and potential scope of the alternative supplier search is shown in Fig. 3.M.

(continued)

Finding : *Four of the Six sub categories are supplied by three or more current suppliers.*

Supplier/Sub-category Mix
(% of total sub-category sales volume)   Fuses

Supplier	DIN	HRC/BS88	Porcelain	Semi-conductor	Service	Accessories & bases	Supplier total
GEC Alsthom	17.8%	66.6%		67.8%	71.6%	49.7%	57.5%
Siemens	82.0%	27.8%		32.2%	1.2%	18.1%	24.7%
PDL Industries	0.2%	4.3%	100%		27.2%	32.0%	16.9%
Bell-MEM		1.3%				0.2%	0.9%
Sub category total	100%	100%	100%	100%	100%	100%	100%

Potential opportunity for supplier consolidation.

Fig. 3.J Category performance analysis

Finding : *Purchase value and trade margins achieved within each subcategory differ significantly.*

Supplier/Sub-category Purchases[1]
($m, FY97)   Fuses

Supplier	DIN	HRC/BS88	Porcelain	Semi-conductor	Service	Accessories & bases	Supplier total
GEC Alsthom	0.023	0.888		0.086	0.176	0.316	1.489
Siemens	0.082	0.347		0.095	0.002	0.065	0.591
PDL Industries	Negligible	0.104	0.286		0.157	0.119	0.666
Bell-MEM		0.03					0.03
Sub category total	0.105	1.369	0.286	0.181	0.335	0.5	2.776

Notes: (1) Supplier purchases = Sales $ less TM $, does not include rebates, discounts etc.

Fig. 3.K Category performance analysis

(continued)

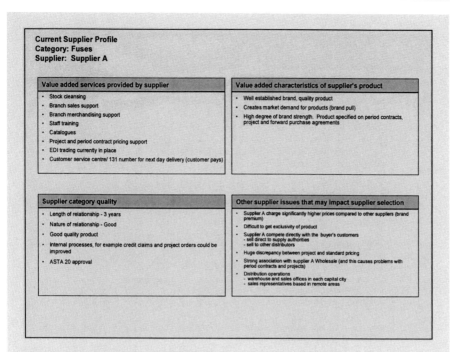

Fig. 3.L Supplier strengths and weaknesses

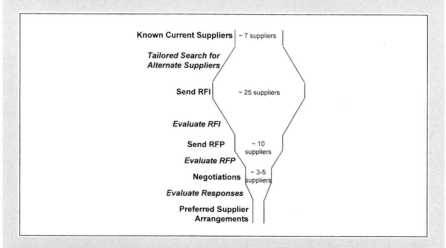

Fig. 3.M Alternate supplier search approach

(continued)

The category, customer and supplier analysis demonstrated above not only can support the negotiation process but also pinpoint areas that need improvement. They uncover areas for potential opportunities with set questions involving the seven opportunity areas shown in Fig. 3.N.

Opportunity Area	Questions To Be Asked	Savings
Purchasing Process	• Are there quantity discounts or price breaks? Are we taking advantage of them? • Should we buy direct from the manufacturer or through a distributor? • Can we consolidate volume across divisions? Across suppliers? Across SKUs?	• Price Discounts
Distribution / Logistics	• Are we utilising our resources effectively? Should we centralise distribution? • Where should the slow-moving items be located? • Who is paying for freight?	• Inventory Carrying Cost • Freight • Distribution
Trading Terms	• How long do we have to pay? • Are there discounts for early payment? • Are there rebates? • What is the policy for returns?	• Cost of Capital • Rebates
Price Discrepancies	• Are there significant differences between current and potential supplier prices? • Can we index supplier prices to an objective, verifiable source? • Do supplier cost structures differ?, Why? • Are there opportunities to conduct internal price benchmarking?	• Price discounts • Cost savings
Product Specifications	• Are there packaging issues? What problems do these cause? • Are we over specifying products? • Can we change/impact industry specifications? • How strong is the brand? • Can we offer our own brand as an alternate?	• Product simplification • Cost savings
Customers	• Do any individual customers have any specific requirements that may impact sourcing? • Do customer segments have specific sourcing requirements? • Are a few customers driving most of the volume? How does this impact sourcing?	• Improved customer service • Product/ inventory savings • Purchasing efficiencies
Volume Consolidation	• Can we reduce the number of suppliers? • Are there opportunities to consolidate volume across the buyer's divisions? • Can we shift volume (or part of the volume) between suppliers and change the supplier volume mix? • Can we rationalise sku's? • Can sku's be substituted?	• Fewer suppliers • Preferred suppliers • Administration savings • Volume related cost savings

Fig. 3.N Opportunities for savings

Strategic Sourcing: Expenditure Category Strategy Formulation

4

Abstract

Each procure input has a different strategic implication to the company; hence it requires a different strategic approach in procuring these individual inputs. When developing an appropriate approach management must first, gaging the criticality of the input as well as the complexity of the supply market. Second, it must identify levers for achieving the success of procuring the inputs. Third, it must choose most appropriate strategic sourcing options, ranging from outsourcing to insourcing. This chapter presents the framework for formulating procurement strategy for each expenditure category.

Keywords

Outsourcing • Input criticality • Category strategy • Souring management • Supply management • Material management • Procurement approach

4.1 Expenditure Category Strategy

Expenditure category strategy formulation represents the second major step in strategic sourcing. A company's strategy defines the nature of its relationships with suppliers and approach to negotiations on each expenditure category, depending on category and industry characteristics.

The strategic sourcing model, illustrated in Fig. 4.2, provides a framework for adopting this strategic approach. It ranks items according to how critical a category is to ensure the ongoing success of the buyer's operations and business profitability, as well as how important the category is to customers. The model also measures the complexity of the supply market, including the level of supplier industry complication, the complexity of supplier relationships and ownership structure and the difficulty in dealing with suppliers and the degree to which suppliers are also competitors (see Fig. 4.1 for assessing the two TSC axes). Combining these two

© Springer Science+Business Media Singapore 2016

S. Parniangtong, *Supply Management*, Management for Professionals,

DOI 10.1007/978-981-10-1723-0_4

Axis	Elements	Rating	N/A	Rationale
Criticality of Category	Product importance to business success	L ⋯⋯⋯⋯⋯⋯⋯⋯⋯⋯⋯⋯⋯⋯ H		
	Importance of product to customer	L ⋯⋯⋯⋯⋯⋯⋯⋯⋯⋯⋯⋯⋯⋯ H		
	Category creates further sales opportunities	L ⋯⋯⋯⋯⋯⋯⋯⋯⋯⋯⋯⋯⋯⋯ H		
	Product is part of core offering	L ⋯⋯⋯⋯⋯⋯⋯⋯⋯⋯⋯⋯⋯⋯ H		
	Overall	L ⋯⋯⋯⋯⋯⋯⋯⋯⋯⋯⋯⋯⋯⋯ H		
Complexity of Supply Market	Degree of supplier fragmentation	L ⋯⋯⋯⋯⋯⋯⋯⋯⋯⋯⋯⋯⋯⋯ H		
	Price volatility	L ⋯⋯⋯⋯⋯⋯⋯⋯⋯⋯⋯⋯⋯⋯ H		
	Supplier is a competitor	L ⋯⋯⋯⋯⋯⋯⋯⋯⋯⋯⋯⋯⋯⋯ H		
	Length of supply chain	L ⋯⋯⋯⋯⋯⋯⋯⋯⋯⋯⋯⋯⋯⋯ H		
	Overall	L ⋯⋯⋯⋯⋯⋯⋯⋯⋯⋯⋯⋯⋯⋯ H		

Fig. 4.1 Element for rating the two axis of sourcing model

axes creates four separate sourcing quadrants. The quadrants are critical in determining what approach should be taken to source items that fall within these conceptual spaces.

4.2   The Four Sourcing Quadrants

Strategic sourcing model illustrated in Figs. 4.2 and 4.3 show how linking a resource's importance with the market's complexity dictates the type of sourcing arrangement and procurement options that should be put in place. Analyzing an organization's requirements in this way identifies the most appropriate relationship and purchasing method for a particular item. Items with low importance, market complexity and financial impact belong in the purchasing management quadrant. Management may establish a purchasing process that minimizes the attention through mechanized order processing (like automatic pilot or vendor managed). The upper far right quadrant represents purchasing items in a high value, highly complex category. These should be managed through strategic partnerships, requiring management to focus on managing suppliers.

Items in the lower far right quadrant are highly available, like commodities, and should be leveraged in order to maximize the company's cost advantage. The strategic focus for items in this quadrant should be in material management to minimize inventory. The upper far left quadrant represents low-value items with a highly complex market. Efficient management of the procurement process can be best achieved through securing supply through long-term contracts with vendors.

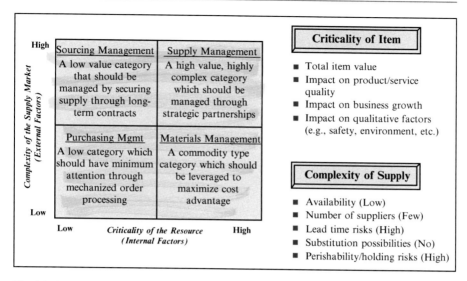

Fig. 4.2 Expenditure category strategic approach

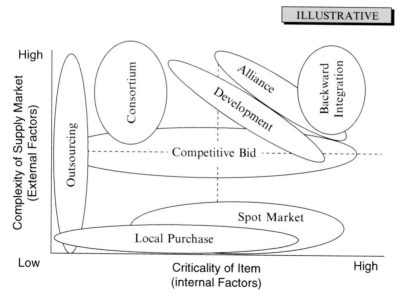

Fig. 4.3 Procurement options

After all items to be purchased are placed in the appropriate strategic approach quadrants, management may choose to implement specific procurement techniques displayed in the strategic procurement options portfolio. These vary in terms of procurement focus, supplier, implementation timeframe and level of sophistication (see Fig. 4.4). Figure 4.5 shows an example of how a company may map its expenditure categories. Details on each procurement option are presented below:

	Purchasing Management	Materials Management	Sourcing Management	Supply Management
Procurement Focus	Non-critical items	Leverage items	Bottleneck items	Strategic items
Sources	Local suppliers	Multiple suppliers, chiefly local	Mostly new national suppliers	National suppliers
Timeframe	Up to 12 months	12 to 24 months	Variable	Long-term
Supply	Abundant	Abundant	Production-based scarcity	Natural scarcity
Decision Authority	Decentralized	Decentralized, but centrally coordinated	Centralized with local releases	Centralized
Main Tasks	Product standardization; inventory optimization	Exploitation of purchasing power; product substitution	Volume insurance; security of inventories	Accurate demand forecasting; long-term relationships
Decision Level	Lower level (e.g., buyer)	Medium level (e.g., chief buyer)	Higher levels (e.g., department heads)	Top level (e.g., Director of Purchasing)

Increasing Levels of Sophistication ▷

Fig. 4.4 Comparison of procurement options

4.3   Strategic Sourcing Options

Based on an elaborated expenditure category analysis, a panoramic view of all expenditure categories is presented by mapping them along two dimensions (internal and external factors). Strategic approaches are formulated for each expenditure category depending on the complexity of the market and criticality of the category. We can now put these strategic approaches to work for each expenditure category by considering several strategic sourcing options. This section details each strategic sourcing option including advantages and disadvantages of each option.

Outsourcing   Outsourcing is when a buyer establishes a contractual agreement for a third party to administer and deliver supplies.[1] The contracts are typically long-term arrangements that require management to continually monitor the third party's performance. For example, a company may outsource office supply management to a third party like Boise Cascade. Under the outsourcing agreement, Boise Cascade will monitor office supply inventory levels and perform other functions to ensure that supplies are available. Once initial inventory needs are established and the program is underway, orders will be generated automatically to replenish supplies or the inventory will be vendor-managed to allow the buyer or purchasing agent to spend more time on strategic purchasing needs. Outsourcing offers several benefits,

---

[1] Martha Craumer, How to Think Strategically About Outsourcing, Harvard Management Update, May 2002.

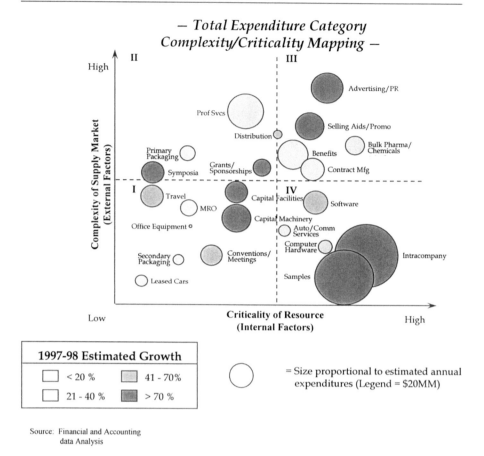

Fig. 4.5 Mapping expenditure categories

such as simplifying the materials management function. This gives management more time to focus on core competencies.

In addition, this allows the third party to consolidate purchasing volume to bargain for lower prices. However, management may lose control if service levels are not met. Outsourcing can be implemented in various ways. Vendor managed replenishment (VMR), in which the vendor is responsible for monitoring and replenishing inventory, has recently become more popular.[2]

Local Purchase This option is most appropriate for products with less market complexity that are not very important. The centerpiece of local purchasing is decentralizing the authority to purchase the product to allow for maximum flexibil-

---

[2] Joseph R. Carter, William J. Markham, and Robert M. Monczka, Procurement Outsourcing—Is it right for you?, Supply Chain Management Review, May/June 2006.

ity. A local office can then buy the product when it is needed. The most widely used tool for accommodating this process is procurement cards for individual expenditures. Procurement cards are issued to authorized personnel throughout the office to purchase specific products. This allows management to keep track of expenditures without scarifying flexibility. A downside to this approach is that it makes professional procurement skills unnecessary, which makes purchasing biased towards personal relationships. To counter this, a firm needs a well-defined hierarchy for authorizing purchases and other measures to better balance the auditing function. Local purchasing can also be done through authorizing local personnel to issue purchase orders. The purchased items are then treated under petty cash accounts.

Spot Market   This approach involves buying commodities at the point of need at the lowest available market prices. Spot buying is widely used in the food processing industry, where commodity-style inactive ingredients are bought in the commodity market. A commodity exchange provides the manufacturer an opportunity to offset transactions, and thus protect to some extent against price and exchange risk. The most common way to do this is through hedging. A hedging contract involves a simultaneous purchase and sale in two different markets. The assumption is that a loss in one market will be offset by an equal gain in the other. If hedging is used, a company may need substantial financial skills, market research and other professional research support. Hedging can occur only where futures trading is possible; not all commodities are traded in the futures market. This approach requires limited planning and leaves the company with the option of forwarding options to buy on good deals.

Competitive Bidding   This option is by far the most commonly used by both business and government to procure products and services. Traditionally, this process begins with defining the product or service requirements to be procured and proceeds with the Request For Proposal (RFP) that is made available to potential bidders. In some cases, the buyer may specify minimum bidder qualifications. Only bidders that meet the qualifications will receive the RFP. Subsequent to reviewing the proposals, the buyer will enter several rounds of negotiations with more than one qualified bidder. This makes negotiation skills and other supporting systems—such as a database containing detailed information on specific bidders and the competitive nature of the market on specific products—crucial to the success of the negotiation process. This bidding process has several advantages and disadvantages. The process generally stirs the negotiation process to focus only on unit price with a little focus on what both sides can do to eliminate inefficiencies in the process, yielding mutual benefits. Other disadvantages include a lack of loyalty from both sides and the potential that both sides would lock themselves into higher prices for longer than necessary. By the same token, long-term contracts allow both sides to plan ahead and manage the supply chain network to accommodate the transactions. In addition, contracts that lock in prices over time reduce volatility. Competitive bidding has several variations, such as a totally open bid, a bid open to only preferred vendors or a partnership with a bid as an audit.

Consortium When market complexity for an expenditure category is high but the importance of the product to the buyer is relatively low, an individual buyer may not be able to negotiate effectively with powerful sellers due to low purchase volume. The alternative for the buyer is to pool purchasing needs with other companies. This would increase the purchased volume and should result in lower costs and better service terms for the consortium. For example, a pharmaceutical company may form a consortium consisting of non-competitor members to jointly buy chemicals from a large chemical producer. The success of this approach depends heavily on a buyer's ability to assemble a consortium with appropriate members and develop procedures for purchasing that meet all consortium needs. The disadvantages of this option include the difficulty of finding non-competitors with similar buying requirements and the complexity of purchase timing and delivery. However, forming a consortium provides several advantages. First and foremost, it substantially increases the leverage of individual buyers, resulting in a greater likelihood the firms can get the vendor's attention and buy the necessary items.

Development For vital expenditure categories with high market complexity, the company has several options for procurement. These include supplier development, backward integration and alliance—all of which are by far more complicated and require a higher level of sophistication. Hence higher management involvement is crucial to their success. When considering the use of supplier development, management may begin by identifying a few marginal suppliers whose objectives could be tied in with the firm's objectives. For example, a drug-making company may identify a handful of small drug innovators that specialize in developing new drugs that are aligned with the company's objective to broaden specific product lines. Thereafter, the company may consider investing in these selected companies (such as investing in the joint-purchase of specific assets). The success of supplier development programs hinges largely on joint development programs with dedicated resources, the executive leadership sponsoring the program and business interactions between the two parties. The supplier development option allows a company to gain substantial influence over a supplier's business, pricing and cost improvements. However, this option has some disadvantages. For example, it requires substantial amounts of capital and time, it may incur potential risk in developing target suppliers and the relationship may affect relationships with other suppliers that are not being targeted for development.

Alliance Forming an alliance with suppliers is another option for management to procure items in the far upper-right hand corner of the sourcing model. In an alliance, companies seek to jointly engage in initiatives in order to mutually enhance their revenue. In general, an alliance may be arranged in two forms: Contractual and equity. For example, a company may seek to form a jointly operated raw materials packaging operation in the supplier's production facility. A more detailed arrangement under this option is shown in Fig. 4.6. The alliance option requires about as much attention from upper management as the development option. However, with some form of alliance, a company should be able to lower costs across the supply chain. If all participants can work out a benefits-sharing arrangement, then they can

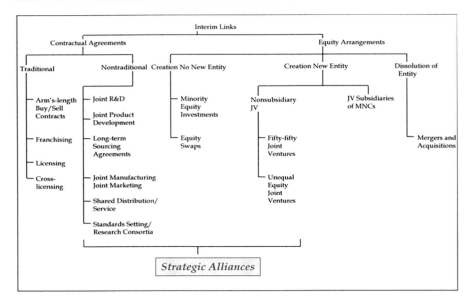

Fig. 4.6 Contractual arrangement in forming the alliance

reach a higher level of stability in the relationship and improvements in service, as well as access to tangential benefits on marketing information, product design and others. Management may encounter several disadvantages when choosing this option, such as difficulties in structuring the most effective arrangements with a reduced number of participants, as well as some negative impacts to relationships with non-allied supply chain participants.

Backward Integration   Backward integration is when the company buys the supplier's equity. This option offers the ultimate level of stability since the company has total control of all aspects of the supplier's operations. Additionally, this option creates barriers for competitors to gain access to raw materials and services from the acquired supplier. This option by far requires the highest level of capital and reduces the company's flexibility in making major changes in sourcing. For example, a well-integrated brewery company that owns container companies (bottles, cans) may be slow to react to a new container process (like plastic) since adopting the new container would jeopardize its own container business. Another disadvantage is that acquiring a new business may drain highly talented personnel into learning something new. Backward integration requires high levels of executive involvement and leadership in making the decision, as well as execution. Very often, outsiders are sought to perform an independent assessment of how the two companies match up and estimate the value of the integration effort.

	OUTSOURCING	LOCAL PURCHASE	SPOT	COMPETITIVE BIDDING	CONSORTIUM	DEVELOPMENT	ALLIANCE	BACKWARD INTEGRATION
DEFINITION	Contracting for a third-party to administer and deliver supply needs	Decentralized purchasing at time of need	Buying commodity goods at point of need at correct market prices	Traditional request for bid process	Pooling purchasing needs with other companies	Investment in marginal supplier to tie to firm's objectives	Joint revenue efforts, with or without equity interests	Acquisition of supply base
EXAMPLE	Boise Cascade prepares stocks and monitors office supplies	Use of procurement cards for individual expenditures	Commodity-style inactive ingredient purchases in the market	Many Current practices.	Buying chemicals jointly with a non-comp pharma company	Investment in small drug innovator	Jointly operated raw material/ packaging operation in production facility	Acquisition
TIME FRAME	Typically long-term	Immediate	Transactional	Periodic (~1/2–3 Years)	Variable	Long-Term	Long-Term	Perpetual
LEVEL OF PROCESS CONTROL	Moderate	Low	Very Low	High	Moderate/ High	High	High	Very High
EXPOSURE AND MARKET RISK	Moderate/High	High	Very High*/Low	Moderate/ High****	Low/Moderate	Low/Moderate	Low/Moderate	Very Low
EXPOSURE TO BUSINESS RISK	Low***	Low/Moderate	High*/ Moderate**	Low/Moderate	Low	High	Moderate	Very High
KEY OPERATING MODEL REQUIREMENTS	Robust, "open" systems · Strong performance managers/ monitoring process · Careful assessment of core competencies	Well-defined hierarchy for purchasing · Balanced audit function · Ease-of-use support tools (e.g., PC point of use, PC cards, etc.)	Strong market research capability · Financial analysis skills · Commodities exchange relationships · Superior information systems	Fact-based negotiating skills and supporting processes · Highly automated vendor tracking and analysis · Superior organizational negotiating skills	Executive assemblies · "Membership" representatives · Development of executional procedures for purchasing and fulfillment	Executive leadership/ sponsorship · Business interaction assessment · Joint development program with dedicated resources · Objective of moving to alliance	Executive leadership/ sponsorship · Business interaction assessment · "Exchange" program · Tightly tied processes and systems	Initial executive leadership · Independent validation of fit/value · Redesign/ refinement of network

Complexity/Sophistication

Fig. 4.7 Portfolio of strategic sourcing options

		OUTSOURCING	LOCAL PURCHASE	SPOT	COMPETITIVE BIDDING	CONSORTIUM	DEVELOPMENT	ALLIANCE	BACKWARD INTEGRATION
Advantages		· Dramatic reduction in complexity · Increased ability to focus on core competencies · Third-party achieves greater volume buys · Cost reductions · Typically, service improvements	· Simple · Responsive · Cost effective within certain parameters	· Limited planning requirements · Ability to forward buy on good deals	· Locks in price over time horizon reducing volatility · Improves ability to plan and manage network	· Increases leverage substantially · Allows visibility into others' purchasing histories · Greater likelihood of vendor attention and buy-in · Typically, cost reductions and service improvement	· Ability to move to alliance status · Substantial influence over supplier pricing · Cost and service improvements	· Reduced cost across supply chain ("gain sharing") · Stability · Improved service levels · Access to tangential benefits – Design – Market information – Improvement opportunities	· Ultimate stability · Low market risk · High degree of control · Barrier to competitors
Disadvantages		· Loss of control if service levels not met · Need to carefully evaluate contractual commitments · Requires improved internal discipline (sometimes)	· Need for establishment and audit of authority levels · Lack of involvement of professional procurement skills · Bias toward personal relationships	· If unhedged significant market risk · If hedged, requires substantial financial skills and professional research support · Minimal ability to optimally design supply · Negates network planning efforts	· Focuses only a unit price, not looking at "gain sharing" opportunity · Potential to lock in high price · Resource intensive · Limits loyalty	· Difficulty finding non-competitors with similar buys/require ments · Time/effort to form coalition · Complexity of buy timing and delivery · Fragility of coalition	· Need for investment – time – capital · Potential business risk in target supplier · Possibility of affecting short-term relations with other vendors	· Difficulty of structuring most effective arrangement · Limited number of alliances that can be supported – # vendors – # types · Impact on non-alliance relationships	· Asset intensive · May be outside of core competency, focus or requiring raw talent · Reduces flexibility
Variations		· Vendor managed replenishment (VMR) · Point-of-use requisition	· Procurement card · Local PO · Petty cash	· Hedged · Pure spots	· Preferred vendor base · Totally open bid (e.g., TPN) · Partnership with bid as audit	· Consortium with alliance · Consortium with bidding	See previous page	See previous page	· Asset purchase · Total acquisition

Fig. 4.8 Advantages/disadvantages of strategic sourcing options

The strategic sourcing model provides a framework for organizations to determine its highest priority needs according to overall corporate objectives. This can determine which needs should be given the most time and resources within sourcing operations. Such an approach can reduce the total costs of procurement, increase sales, reduce lead times and improve the company's overall competitive advantage. Figures 4.7 and 4.8 summarize the procurement options mentioned above.

Strategic Sourcing: The Supplier Strategy

5

Abstract

All suppliers are not created equal. They vary depending on their capabilities, experience and strategic focuses (Jeffrey H. Dyer and Nile W. Hatch, Using supplier networks to learn faster, MIT Sloan Review, Spring 2004, Vol. 45, No. 3). This represents another challenge when having to identify, select and formulate negotiation terms with the suppliers. This chapter presents the framework for determining appropriate number of suppliers, approaches for choosing suppliers and negotiation focuses.

Keywords

Supplier strategy • Souring best practices • Vendor management

5.1 The Supplier Strategy Model

The supplier strategy model helps determine the overall approach to sourcing key expenditures, including the number of suppliers and focus of negotiations. The model consists of two axes: the first represents the level of product complexity, and the second defines the level of market freedom in the expenditure category.[1] Product complexity refers to the degree of knowledge required to source, manage and use the product, as well as the product's uniqueness. Categories with low complexity may be commodities. The level of market freedom represents the level of competition and/or fragmentation within the supply market and the magnitude of costs involved in switching between suppliers. As the level of competition

---

[1] Jefrey H. Dyer, Doug Sung Cho, and Wujin Chu, Strategic Supplier Segmentation, California Management Review, Vol. 40, No. 2, Winter 1998.

© Springer Science+Business Media Singapore 2016
S. Parniangtong, *Supply Management*, Management for Professionals,
DOI 10.1007/978-981-10-1723-0_5

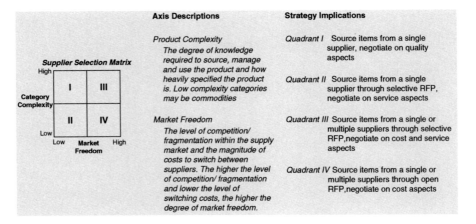

Fig. 5.1 Axis components of supplier selection

Axis	Elements	Rating		N/A	Rationale
	Knowledge required to source product	L	H		
	Level of product/technical specifications	L	H		
Category Complexity	Product brand strength	L	H		
	Strategic importance of product	L	H		
	Overall	L	H		
	No of potential suppliers	L	H		
	Supplier switching costs (High cost-low rating)	L	H		
	Ability to switch suppliers	L	H		
Market Freedom	Feasibility of sourcing globally	L	H		
	Relative size of movable volume	L	H		
	Relative buyer size	L	H		
	Overall	L	H		

Fig. 5.2 Rating of the two axis

(more fragmentation) rises and the switching costs drop, the level of market free-dom increases. Figure 5.1 depicts the supplier strategy model, and Fig. 5.2 illus-trates the rating for the two axes.

Quadrant I (upper left) represents items with a high degree of category complex-ity where the buyer has a little market freedom to choose suppliers. The buyer should focus on sourcing items from a single supplier and focus the negotiations on obtaining products of the highest possible quality from the supplier.[2] Items in Quadrant II (lower left) have lower category complexity and market freedom. Hence, the buyer should focus on choosing suppliers via selective RFP to get the

---

[2] Jim Morgan, Just How Good a Customer are You? Purchasing, November 19, 1998.

most competitive supplier. The negotiations should focus on obtaining the highest possible service quality from the selected supplier. Quadrant III represents the most difficult items to source as they are the most complicated but market freedom is relatively high. The buyer must consider a variety of supplier options. In this quadrant, the buyer may source from a single or multiple suppliers through selective RFP. The buyer should concentrate the negotiations on obtaining both the most competitive cost as well as the highest level of service. In Quadrant IV, the buyer has high market freedom to source items with a relatively low level of complexity. The buyer may source the items from a single or multiple suppliers through open bidding and the negotiations should focus on cost.

Best Practices in Strategic Sourcing Tactics

Regardless of the strategic approach and procurement options selected for a given expenditure category, buyers may leverage buying power to ensure that full value is attained. Many leading companies have adopted practices to streamline their procurement process to achieve the maximum value beyond price concessions from suppliers.[3] Some of the following best practices require buyers to work closely with suppliers to achieve the added value, while others are functions that buyers may choose to perform internally. These best practices are grouped under the following three areas:

Vendor Management: Best-practice procurement tactics under this area are designed for a buyer to work in conjunction with suppliers to reduce costs, improve a supplier's performance and achieve the highest product quality. These best practices involve:

- *Supplier program*: Several leading manufacturers (especially OEMs in the automotive industry) have successfully implemented programs that require suppliers to build their operations or warehouses near or next to their production facilities. Shipments from suppliers to an OEM's manufacturing facilities are scheduled frequently with a mixed truck (a truckload of products gathered from many vendors). In many cases, a third party is employed to perform the pick-up with a transportation sweep (also known as milk runs). The success of a supplier program depends heavily on communication between OEMs and suppliers for supplier-managed replenishment, pull replenishment, Advance-Shipping-Notice (ASN) and scheduling just-in-time deliveries for final assembly. As a buyer, the OEM will benefit from reduced material inventory, shorter manufacturing lead times, simplified material replenishment and reduced manufacturing costs.

(continued)

---

[3] Jonathan Hughes, Turn Your Suppliers into Cost-Cutting Allies, Harvard Business School Publishing Corporation, 2005.

- *Supplier base rationalization*: This is the process of evaluating, selecting and consolidating suppliers based on certain performance criteria so a company can find a supplier with whom it can develop a strategic relationship. A set of performance criteria are used to evaluate suppliers and selected suppliers are rewarded with more purchase volume. These criteria may include products that always meet quality specifications, certified suppliers or those that are willing to use certified laboratories and the ability to produce a Certificate of Analysis (COA) prior to receiving goods (in the case of chemical substances). Other performance criteria may include reliability, accuracy and responsiveness. Companies can measure if a supplier always delivers products on time and up to quality expectations; if shipments are always accurate in respect to ASN; if shipments are made in the optimal size and products are pre-mixed or blended when appropriate; and if shipments are made frequently with a minimal lead time. Buyers should expect to benefit from a smaller, more reliable, more responsive supply base, increased on-time deliveries, improved quality of supply, reduced downtimes and improved finished-goods quality.
- *Compliance program*: Compliance programs are a way to measure, communicate and reward or penalize supply base performance, which ultimately can improve the overall supply base. Putting in place a compliance program requires a supplier tracking system to measure a supplier's performance in areas such as on-time delivery, quality, quantity and ASN. The tracking information is summarized and analyzed constantly, and the results are communicated internally and externally. Rewards or recognitions may be given annually to the highest performers (suppliers of the month) and a penalty structure may be put in place to penalize inferior performers. Compliance programs offer similar benefits to those of supply base rationalization.

Buying Approaches: Given the procurement options described earlier, buyers may adopt the specific buying approaches listed below to leverage purchases:

- *3-2-1 consolidation*: This concept focuses on phased consolidation, which applies to highly fragmented buys. The process begins when a company selects three suppliers through open bidding. At the next stage of consolidation, two suppliers are picked out of the three bidders. In the final round, the remaining two suppliers bid for the strategic partnership. This process fully utilizes competition in the supplier selection process. The buys are also fully leveraged, which results in maximum benefits from dealing with the fragmented supplier base.
- *Bundling*: Bundling allows buyers to capitalize on greater buying or transportation leverage. Buyers using suppliers from the same location, region or country can form a consortium (or membership) for pur-

(continued)

chases. Typically, orders are consolidated when the consortium team negotiates with suppliers. Significant benefits can be realized both from material cost savings as well as potential transportation savings—especially in situations that involve many buyers that are independently importing goods.

- *Commodity hedging*: Hedging is a risk-shifting method where individuals and businesses use to transfer the price risk of ownership of commodities or price risk of normal business to those who are willing to carry these risks in return for possible profits.[4] Commodity hedging is used to minimize the effects on probability of fluctuated market prices. Hedging helps minimize the effects of price variations over time. The key benefit from hedging is the reduction in price volatility on the purchased material—especially commodities—that should improve the buyer planning process.

Material Management: Many leading OEMs and final assemblers have successfully implemented material management techniques that emphasize ready-to-use input material and SKU rationalization to improve supply.

- *Ready-to-use*: It is a concept in which materials are delivered both process-ready and quality-ready for line use. Process-ready refers to packaging and container sizes that are ready to feed the final assembly. Buyers are no longer required to break the package or consolidate the package at the point of use. This may also include pre-mixed or blended materials that are ready for use. Quality-ready refers to when materials or products are shipped from certified suppliers with certified laboratories with an advanced COA receipt. Key benefits from the ready-to-use concept are a reduction in inventory, work steps and lead times that should result in cost improvements.

- *Material and/or SKU rationalization*: This is the process of consolidating and simplifying the number of materials and SKUs. The process and analyses requirements are described earlier in this chapter. Benefits include reduced material inventory due to increased cross utilization of specific materials and inventory-associated costs.

---

[4] Kalman I. Perlman, Handbook of Purchasing and Materials Management, Probus Publishing Company, Chicago, Illinois, 1992.

Strategic Sourcing: Fact-Based Negotiation (FBN)

6

Abstract

Fact-based negotiation is a process for seeking a win-win outcome in negotiating in procuring specific category of inputs. It is based on two fundamental principle of collaboration and leverage bargaining that are guided by facts through a series of analyses. This chapter details a step-by-step approach in performing a fact-based negotiation. It includes negotiation tactics that will allow buyers to persuade the suppliers to comply with the negotiated deals.

Keywords

Fact-based negotiation • Negotiation tactic • Supplier response • Negotiation planning • Supplier selection • Supplier measurement

6.1 Fact-Based Negotiation

Fact-based negotiation is intended to arm the negotiating team with any and all facts necessary to reach a desired outcome. The process consists of the following four sub-processes:

- Negotiation strategy and case building
- Supplier response and positioning
- Negotiation planning, discussion and resolution
- Supplier evaluation

Details of each sub-process are given below.

© Springer Science+Business Media Singapore 2016
S. Parniangtong, *Supply Management*, Management for Professionals,
DOI 10.1007/978-981-10-1723-0_6

6.1.1 Negotiation Strategy and Case Building

This sub-process begins with selecting compelling facts to determine the leverage points of both the buyer and supplier and strategies for countering the supplier's leverage points. The buyer can then shape the negotiation's goals and objectives to involve defining a Least Acceptable Solution (LAS), Maximum Supportable Solution (MSS) and Best Alternative (BA). This sub-process includes developing a strategy for switching to a new supplier (see Fig. 6.1).

Conceptually, negotiations are approached through two extreme strategies: collaborative and leveraged bargaining. Most negotiations will most likely fall in the middle of the two extremes. A collaborative negotiation takes a non-confrontational, problem-solving and collaborative approach to develop multiple options to find an option that yields to principle, not pressure. Leveraged bargaining is about hard bargaining on concrete facts with the goal of winning or breaking even. The buyer's relative leverage can be used to predict how close it will come to achieving MSS. The matrix shown in Fig. 6.2 can help define the negotiation approach that is best suited for an individual situation.[1]

Based on internal data, analyses and category strategy, a buyer should be able to determine the advantages it can exploit during the negotiation process. These advantages can build around a much larger purchased volume relative to the supplier's production capacity; purchasing a commodity-like goods that has many suppliers; and the potential increase in purchasing volume in the future.

The industry and supplier knowledge obtained from a supply industry structure analysis, industry structure analysis and the supplier's customer buying practices allows the buyer to develop a list of advantages that suppliers may try to leverage. For example, a supplier may justify higher prices by offering higher quality standards, knowing that the cost of switching suppliers is too high or realizing that a buyer has only a few good suppliers to choose from.

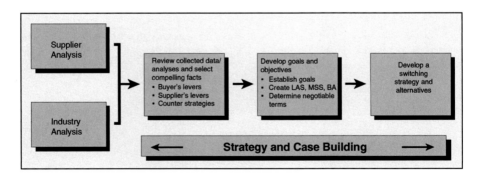

Fig. 6.1 The strategy and case building process

---

[1] Andrew Cox, Paul Ireland, Chris Lonsdale, Joe Sanderson, Glyn Watson, Supply Chain Management: A Guide to Best Practice, FT Prentice Hall, 2003.

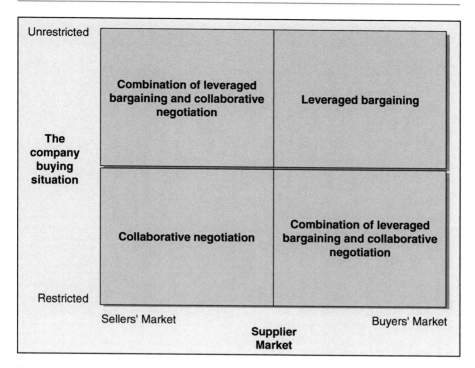

Fig. 6.2 Negotiation matrix

   To counter this leverage, buyers must develop some creative techniques. If possible, these counter levers should be built into the negotiation process so that the supplier becomes aware of the buyer's position. Figure 6.3 shows a leverage example.

   Once the levers are determined, a buyer should develop goals and objectives for the negotiation. Particularly essential are the buyer's LAS, MSS and BA. LAS is the absolute bottom line that the buyer would accept when coming out of the final negotiations. In defining the LAS, the buyer should not settle for anything less as it would hurt the business. MSS is the altogether best proposal that supports the buyer's business interests. The buyer should keep in mind that one will never get more than it asks for, and aspiration is one of the most important factors in determining success. Therefore, in defining MSS, the buyer should be ambitious but have a defensible rationale. It is also important to understand that MSS is independent of what the other party will accept and is merely an opening proposal. One way to differentiate LAS from MSS is to think of the differences between a company's "wants" and "needs" as shown in Fig. 6.4. BA is the course of action the buyer will pursue if the supplier is not willing to agree to the bottom line. A BA is a unilateral action on the buyer's part. Defining the BA will help the buyer realistically assess its relative power, become more flexible and ensure that it will not settle at any cost. From the buyer's perspective, it is possible to determine LAS, MSS and BA for

Buyer's Strategic Levers	Supplier A Strategic Levers	Buyer's Counter Levers
• Buyer is a large volume buyer • This is a commodity purchase, many suppliers exist • Buyer is interested in long term supplier partnering • Buyer has vast knowledge of the supplier's industry, competitors and key price drivers • Buyer is a stable, growing business, who will increase their purchases over time	• Buyer is a small part of the supplies's business • Supplier A has higher quality standards justifying higher price • There are few good suppliers to choose from • Buyer's switching costs are too high • Buyer has too few options on this purchase	• The majority of their buyers are Buyer's size • Buyer is committed to training another supplier • Buyer should see increased competition, especially in terms of value-added services • Buyer is committed to taking calculated risks to further the business • Buyer can potentially outsource the entire purchase to a third party or further integrate the process if required

Fig. 6.3 Leverage example

Least Acceptable Solution 'Needs'		Maximum Supportable Solution 'Wants'
• Maximum acceptable price that meets profit goals	⟷	• Minimum price in the market
• Market advantage delivery time	⟷	• Shortest delivery time possible
• Product performance to meet specifications	⟷	• Performance exceeding specifications
• Price firm for one year	⟷	• Longer term price guarantee

Fig. 6.4 LAS and MSS definition

each of the key buying criteria. For example, product quality, delivery and price may have different requirements for LAS, MSS and BA.

The buyer should develop a strategy for switching to a new supplier during this sub-process. In developing a switching strategy, the company should perform a cost-benefit analysis to consider factors such as learning curve, time required to switch back if required, risks to the buyer's customers, impact to the buyer's internal operations and the resources required to mitigate the impact.

6.1.2   Supplier Response and Positioning

This sub-process arms the buyer with the ability to anticipate supplier responses and map out negotiation tactics to counter them. Suppliers will respond by objecting to the FBN process in general and raising issues related to financial costs. The responses will include: "Indices and cost structures are averages and don't apply to us"; "We have a better quality product that requires us to charge more"; "What's in it for us?"; and "Implementing the buyer's way of doing business is costing us thousands". It is imperative to have prepared uniform answers to these responses before the formal negotiation process begins. The following are negotiating tactics that will help persuade the supplier when negotiating a deal:

6.1.2.1 Use Competitive Leverage
This tactic involves entering a negotiation with alternative suppliers and alternative products. It is important to first establish credibility with the supplier with information like the company's size and capacity, historical precedent and the desire for a long-term relationship. This tactic works well when the buyer can convince the supplier that its demand will be met, thus enhancing the value of the supplied product. The buyer must present a confident, self-assured team that fully understands the information, issues, products and applications.

- *Framing*: This is the process of defining a negotiation's reference points to promote a favorable outcome. The current arrangement becomes a neutral point, and the initiated position will define the endpoint for the discussions. Figure 6.5 depicts two different initiation points that become reference points for the negotiations that will lead to two different expected results. It is important for the buyer to be proactive in framing the negotiations with prospective suppliers.

Information Information is the single most powerful factor in negotiations. A buyer that is well versed in the facts and arguments will drive the outcome of a negotiating session. In addition, a strong presentation of the research sends a message to the supplier that any incomplete arguments brought forward will not stand up in the negotiation process. Finally, the supplier's information will be reviewed for completeness and accuracy before it can influence any procurement decisions. It is always better to provide only necessary information when required and show little emotion; avoid acting surprised.

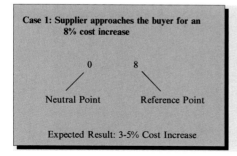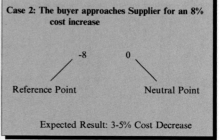

Fig. 6.5 Framing example

Deadlines Take a proactive approach in structuring the timeframe for completing negotiations. The buyer should determine the timeframe to allow ample time for research to build its case.

Limited Authority This is when a negotiating party says a third party will not allow them to concede a particular point even if they would like to do so. A similar tactic involves presenting a representative who has the authority to negotiate but then changing the key decision-maker after reaching a tentative agreement.

Supplier Threat Not to Ship Goods A threat not to ship supplies for current requirements will be met with disdain. Threatening to void existing arrangements is not a bargaining chip and is beyond the realm of professional and ethical standards. The buyer should insist that current agreements are shipped on time. If the supplier so wishes, the buyer should negotiate a mutually agreeable plan for ending the relationship with respect to future business.

Single Issue Bargaining This is a supplier tactic for negotiating a cost increase based on increasing one cost element. While cost improvements may be more than offset the increases, suppliers are likely to present only the costs that are rising.

What's Your Theory? This is when a party questions the logic behind an initial proposal. The supplier must then state explicitly the information and assumptions that went into developing the request. Challenging the supplier's facts, calculations, assumptions or methods will weaken their resolve and lower their expectations.

Concessions This involves knowing which terms are least important to the buyer and trading them for concessions that have value. When preparing for negotiations, buyers should identify concessions that can be granted within "the buyer's way". For example, if the buyer plans to promote a supplier's product, it can expect a concession from the supplier by making this part of the bargaining process. It is always better to create a hierarchy of concessions from "wants" to "needs" and try to make concessions slowly by matching the concessions with those of other party.

Confusion This tactic avoids addressing a contentious issue through creating confusion or steering all discussions away from the point at hand.

Non-valuable Concessions A buyer should identify supplier concessions that have a little or no value to it and relay that information to the supplier.

BATNA This is an acronym for Best Alternative To A Negotiated Agreement. This is the point at which the buyer invokes a switching strategy. Identifying the BATNA requires in-depth research to develop plans for switching suppliers in the event that a negotiated agreement cannot be reached. While the buyer can tell the supplier it has a switching strategy, it should never reveal the details of its BATNA.

Brinkmanship   This tactic is used to identify the supplier's BATNA by challenging the existing perception of the balance of power. The buyer conducting the negotiations must recognize that the supplier's best offer will only come when it knows the buyer is prepared to switch suppliers.

Perceived Flexibility   This tactic is when the buyer presents a supplier with a limited set of alternatives that are crafted to provide the buyer with a favorable agreement regardless of the supplier's decision. As a result, the supplier feels it has more control over the negotiations when presented with a choice.

Detail Management   This when a buyer volunteers to write up the agreement after the major terms have been agreed upon so the details are favorable to it. In many agreements, a few points that can have a significant impact on the whole agreement are ambiguous or excluded.

Strategic Silence   This tactic is useful for getting a supplier to expound on a statement or position by not responding to it in any manner. The supplier will feel an obligation to fill the silence with details or an explanation. The buyer can then use these details to develop a response.

Power of Reward   This involves making an offer to provide the supplier with terms that are beneficial in the future in return for concessions in the current agreement. The buyer may share certain details of the corporate strategic plan and how it will lead to new opportunities or better terms for the supplier.

Personalize the Issue   Personal relationships can influence negotiations, and team members should be aware that suppliers will likely appeal to these relationships when requesting concessions. The buyer must not allow this tactic to influence its judgment. However, the buyer may employ this tactic when formal discussions have stalled.

Saving Face   This allows a supplier an easy out at the tail end of a negotiation. The buyer should stress the supplier's good business judgment in striking a deal and appease any emotional issues that might prevent or complicate how the agreement is structured. The buyer should avoid putting the supplier in a situation where it must back down directly from a strong position.

Emotional Investment   The process of working with the supplier to structure a deal may make the supplier more committed to striking a deal. The more a supplier has invested in the negotiations, the less likely they are to walk away from a proposition. Ask suppliers to review the facts presented and personally present information to the buyer. This will show their commitment and simultaneously emphasize the supplier's vulnerability to loss.

Potential Conflict	**How to Resolve**
■ Lack of response	• Use open-ended questions • Maintain occasional silence • Provide incremental information
■ Disagreement	• Identify alternative benefits • Offer proof • Reevaluate true needs • Make concessions • Focus on issues on which you already agree
■ Skepticism	• Establish trust • Identify with vend or needs • Offer proof • Avoid sarcasm
■ Personality clash	• Don't overreact • Show positive attitude • Don't judge other party • Change team composition
■ Negativity	• Listen actively • Paraphrase and ask for corrections • Acknowledge the feelings but make your point

Fig. 6.6 Potential trouble spots

Although the buyer must familiarize itself with the above tactics and use them selectively, it is almost as important to be aware of potential hurdles or trouble spots. This will allow the buyer to respond effectively to the supplier's negotiation tactics and take control of the negotiation process. The potential trouble spots and ways for dealing with these are summarized in Fig. 6.6.

6.1.3 Negotiation Planning, Discussion and Resolution

The final step of the fact-based negotiation process is to prepare for the actual negotiations by carefully planning out the logistics of the talks. Planning negotiations consist of several tasks for pre-and post-negotiation sessions. On pre-negotiation, the planning process should include the number of meetings and the agenda for each meeting, which suppliers will be taken into the negotiation rounds and which buyer team members will be invited to the meetings.

A successful negotiation will have a different number of engagement rounds, with each round having different objectives and utilizing different techniques. Typically, the first round explains the buyer's situation and provides justifications for cost reductions or profitability improvements. If the number of suppliers is large, the buyer may turn the supplier conference into a forum. The buyer should control the first round briefing, especially the meeting's flow. The buyer must maintain objectivity and a strong commitment to work with qualified suppliers.

In the second round, the parties should discuss the business requirements and how they will be achieved. The buyer should discuss the financial requirements (cost improvement expectations, quality specifications and delivery) and play attention to comments and responses from suppliers. With this knowledge, the buyer should identify real players and redefine its MSS, LAS and BA.

At the third meeting, the parties should reach a final agreement on each of the business requirements. They should ensure that both parties sign off on all business requirements. These agreements should include benchmarks and other key performance indicators, and the frequency for reviewing the performance that will become the basis for future negotiations. At this point, the buyer can re-emphasize its commitment to achieve the task by explaining that it would accept a reasonable price increase if it can be justified. At the end of this round, uncompetitive suppliers should be eliminated and supplier ideas should be incorporated into the buyer's MSS.

In subsequent rounds of negotiation, the buyer should prepare to make orderly concessions to reach an agreement and always be aware of the LAS and BA. It should focus on forming a long-term relationship with specific suppliers and a joint-team effort in solving problems with suppliers. The negotiation rounds and what they focus on are summarized in Fig. 6.7.

Forming a negotiation team is critical to a successful negotiation process. Each member of the negotiating team brings unique skills to the table and is expected to fulfill a specific team need. In general, a negotiating team consists of:

Principal Negotiator Responsible for conducting primary negotiations; does not have regular contact with supplier.

Round	Typical Techniques (May Vary By Supplier)
■ First Round	• Clarify information submitted in response to the RFP/RFQ • Establish each suppliers' specific interests • Explore/test options that favor our interests • Potentially could be accomplished by means of a supplier conference
■ Second Round	• Redefine The buyer's MSS, LAS, & BA • Identify real "players" • Push back aggressively on laggard/unresponsive suppliers
■ Third Round	• Eliminate uncompetitive suppliers • Incorporate best supplier ideas into the buyer's MSS • Drive toward MSS with preferred supplier(s) using maximum available leverage
■ Subsequent Rounds	• Make orderly concessions to reach agreement always being cognizant of our LAS & BA • Form basis for long-term relationship • Engage in problem solving with supplier

Fig. 6.7 Negotiation rounds and their focuses

Internal Information Specialist Possesses a thorough understanding of user requirements, usage volumes, product cost, etc. A representative from the purchasing department generally fills this role.

External Information Specialist Has a thorough understanding of the supplier's situation and competition, market factors and the industry.

Recorder Provides detailed documentation of all discussions, agreements and unresolved issues.

End User Representative from the area where the product will be used within the buyer's organization. This individual provides the perspective of someone who will utilize the purchased product.

Buyer's Executive Member Assumes a support role during negotiations in providing input from upper level management.

In addition to forming a negotiation team, the buyer should profile the supplier's team, including the anticipated role of each attendee. The supplier team member profile should consist of the individual roles and responsibilities, personal benefits from obtaining the buyer's business, decision-making influence and rank in the supplier's organization, the supplier's negotiating style in the past and any predispositions or prejudices.

6.1.4   RFP/RFQ Preparation

The main purpose of RFP/RFQ is to acquire information for negotiations. As a formatted vehicle for information gathering, RFP/RFQ assists the buyer in efficiently finding and processing a large amount of information. Information is necessary for the buyer to gain an insight on individual suppliers with comparable information. This will enable the buyer to create a level playing field for all suppliers. The process of preparing RFP/RFQ consists of:

Supplier Communication Plan This finalizes the list of potential suppliers (both new and existing), determines the approach for communicating with suppliers (e-mail, phone, site visit, supplier conference) and develops a vehicle for monitoring the RFP/RFQ process.

RFP/RFQ Preparation The RPF/RFQ is a structured document that seeks expressions of interest in the buyer's business from potential suppliers. The document forms the basis for defining the buyer's requirements to suppliers and provides a common platform for the buyer to evaluate supplier responses on an "apples-to-apples" basis. At the minimum, the RFP should contain the following sections:

- General Information
- Instructions/Timeline
- Bid Package/RFQ
- Supplier Questionnaire
- Requirements and Evaluation Criteria

Sending RFP/RFQ   A buyer should also figure out the most appropriate way to deliver the RFP/RFQ to each potential supplier. A log may be developed to verify receiving the document and complete the returned documents from suppliers.

6.2   Suppliers Selection and Evaluation

In selecting suppliers, evaluation criteria should be developed at a significant degree of depth. In general, there are three levels of selection criteria: general, operational and cost. General criteria are established to screen the first batch of suppliers who meet the LAS. This may include criteria for assessing the products/services requirements, supplier capacity, geographical coverage and references. The second criteria dive deeper into each qualified supplier's operational capabilities.[2] For example, although the supplier's products/services may meet the requirements, further assessments are needed to determine the design, quality, delivery and other value-added the supplier will provide. The third set of criteria is to focus on cost—total supply cost, not purchase price. Analyzing the total supply cost in the way mentioned earlier is an excellent starting point to determine the evaluation criteria.[3] The three levels of evaluation criteria are shown in Fig. 6.8. The levels to which a buyer will determine the depth of evaluation criteria vary depending on expenditure category. In additional to the TSC criteria, other possible criteria should also be considered (see Fig. 6.9).

Evaluating a supplier's performance requires a complete understanding of the value received from purchasing the products/services. A supplier's performance should be evaluated to verify that it delivered what it promised to deliver. This includes matching point by point the deliverables to the agreement letter, identifying any areas of non-conformance, confirming the nonconformance with the supplier and bringing the situation to a close by correcting the bill or receiving additional services. The next step in evaluating the supplier's performance is taking a critical view of the quality of its work. To do this, a buyer should review the delivered products/services against the MSS. Finally it should evaluate the products/services delivered on how they impact the bottom line. The buyer should assess how the purchased products/services contribute to the buyer's long-term profitability.

---

[2] Morgan L. Swink and Vincent A. Mabert, Product Development Partnership: Balancing the Needs of OEMs and Suppliers, Business Horizon, May-June 2000.

[3] Jonathan Hughes, Turning Your Suppliers into Cost-Cutting Allies, HBR, 2005.

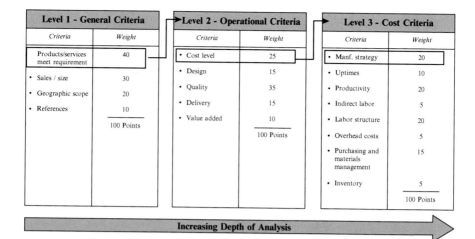

Fig. 6.8   The three levels of evaluation criteria example

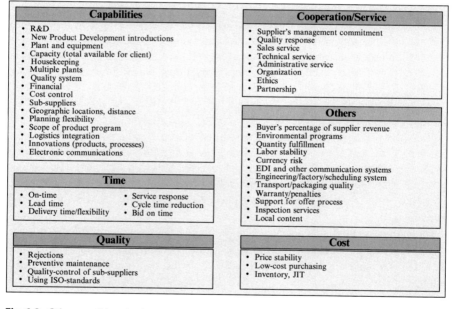

Fig. 6.9   Other possible criteria

Measuring and Evaluating Suppliers

Measuring and evaluating suppliers is an important part of strategic sourcing.

Many quality gurus believe a commitment to total quality should focus on the essence of procurement that measures and manages supplier performance. It has been estimated that supplier nonperformance is more costly than supplier performance management.[4] Best practices in performance measurement call for the buyer to measure a supplier's performance from the total cost perspective, consistently measuring suppliers across expenditure category and geographies. Best practices in supplier performance measurements include:

- Performance measures should lead to buyer satisfaction for both the physical products and the services attached to them. A series of questions illustrated in Fig. 6.10 will help formulate specific measurements.

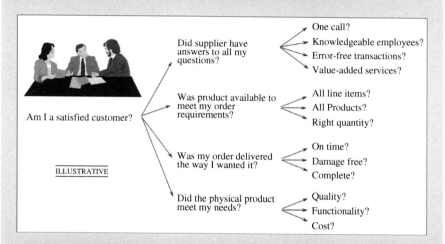

Fig. 6.10 Specifying supplier performance measurement

- Supplier performance measures are needed to assess customer service. The measures include on-time delivery (it is important to recognize that early delivery has penalties and should also be measured), order completeness (fill rate), lead-time (cycle time, measured in days, from issuing purchase order to receipt), flexibility (measured in terms of percent of early reschedules that are accommodated) and other subjective measures like problem responsiveness.

(continued)

---

[4] NAPM Insight, "High Quality Purchasing," May 1992.

- A buyer should measure the entire spectrum of purchased material performance, not just incoming inspection. Additional inspections may include checking material during the process, final inspection, yield, rework, warranty repair and customer returns.
- Formal systems measure internal customer satisfaction by institutionalizing routine feedback on key satisfaction measures. Performance ratings are communicated back to suppliers and issues that need work are addressed jointly with suppliers.
- A buyer should establish formal supplier recognition programs and expand its relationship with recognized suppliers.
- A professional responsible for managing supplier relations should administer a supplier performance measurement system. This includes:
  - The system should enable both the buyer and supplier to quantify progress toward joint goals.
  - Suppliers are given periodic reports showing their own performance and the average for their expenditure group.
  - The measurements are made by a team comprising key personnel who interact with the suppliers and can effectively evaluate them.

When a supplier is the buyer's strategic partner, the following performance measures should be used to assess the supplier's contributions:

- Introduction of new technology from suppliers, new ideas generated.
  - Quantity
  - Quality (subjective)
- Concept-to-customer cycle-time reduction
- Trends that indicate efforts to minimize the introduction of new SKUs, and efforts to standardize their use
- Ease of use or assembly of supplier-designed parts
- Ease of doing business, particularly between a buyer's functional skills and supplier counterparts

It is important to note that both the buyer and supplier must undergo performance evaluations to build a truly solid relationship and sustain mutual benefits. Through soliciting feedback from suppliers, a buyer can receive valuable information on how to be a world-class customer. Motorola practices what they preach about needing excellent suppliers to help them reach their six-sigma quality goal. Here's what they do:

- Each quarter, Motorola sends a survey to suppliers. The responses are kept confidential.
- Suppliers use the survey to rate the performance of each Motorola plant.
- The survey contains 19 areas that are rated on a scale of 1–6.

(continued)

- The first section covers early supplier involvement, the negotiation and award process, schedule sharing, schedule stability and technical support.
- The second section asks suppliers to rate their best customers, excluding Motorola.
  - Motorola uses this information as a benchmark to compare the best customer ratings with their own score.
- (See Fig. 6.11 for a world-class report card.)

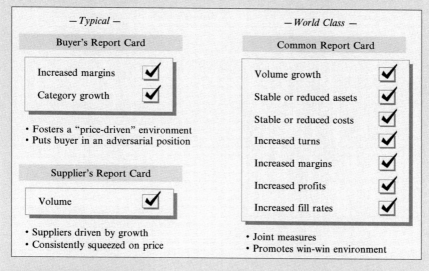

Fig. 6.11 Report card example

Strategic Sourcing: Required Infrastructure of Supply Management

7

Abstract

Strategic sourcing represents a shift in mindset that puts sourcing in the context of how procurement impacts the entire organization—in marketing, sales, research and development and finance. This requires an organization to realign its infrastructure to support strategic sourcing. The internal considerations are organizational structure, the skills needed by staff and management and the strategic sourcing processes. The external factors are supplier management and partnership relationships. Finally, to fully realize the benefits from strategic sourcing from day-to-day operations on up, a company must have the necessary technology to underpin and enable the necessary changes.

Keywords

Organization realignment • Partnership management • Technology enabler

7.1 Realigning Organizational Structure

Traditionally the debate about the purchasing department's role focused on whether purchasing was centralized or decentralized within the organization. But if a company switches to strategic sourcing, then "purchasing" must have a role that spans the organization's operations. This means the purchasing activities should be linked with other departments, as seen in Fig. 7.1. Purchasing interacts with many functional departments, such as manufacturing and marketing. In a sense it acts as the liaison between these departments and the company's suppliers. Without good internal relations between the procurement and user departments, it will be impossible for a company to build strong relationships with external suppliers. The importance of strategic sourcing and its impact on different departments is detailed below:

© Springer Science+Business Media Singapore 2016
S. Parniangtong, *Supply Management*, Management for Professionals,
DOI 10.1007/978-981-10-1723-0_7

Fig. 7.1 Department involved in satisfying purchasing needs

R&D, Engineering and Design Strategic sourcing plays a role in interacting with the R&D department. All executives must understand the products under development and the subsequent purchasing requirements to make the product a success. Strategic sourcing can help ensure that the necessary components of a product's design will be available, affordable and up to the necessary quality standards.

Manufacturing and Operations In order to source the most appropriate goods and materials, the purchasing team must understand issues like quality, scheduling, production time and availability of supply. Strategic sourcing can add value and save money by working with operations to avoid emergency buys, production shutdowns and unscheduled changeovers.

Sales and Marketing By understanding how products are sold to the consumer and at what cost, strategic sourcing can buy goods more effectively. It needs to continually communicate with the sales and marketing teams to understand potential spikes in demand because of promotions or seasonality.

Accounting and Finance Strategic sourcing is the intermediary between accounts payable and the supplier. Paying for items can have a large impact on the company's finance. Therefore, it is important for the strategic sourcing and finance departments to have a good relationship and understand each other's goals and needs. This includes the effects on cash flow and the costs of working capital.

Logistics In any sourcing deal, the buyer tries to not only negotiate for the quality and price of the products but also make the necessary arrangement for receiving a good service as well. Hence logistics arrangement is central to strategic sourcing negotiation. Strategic sourcing needs to communicate and involve logistics to determine how service terms should be negotiated and delivered.

Inventory Management Inventory of the purchased products can represent a significant cost incurred to both buyer and seller if the management of inventory is not addressed properly. Management of physical product inventory directly affects inventory related costs. Hence, how and who will be responsible for monitoring, caring and maintaining a proper level of inventory are central to achieving a strategic sourcing deal.

By ensuring that departments interact across boundaries, a buyer will move purchasing beyond the traditional debate over centralization. In fact, successful strategic sourcing can deliver the benefits of both the centralized and decentralized modes of operation. Strategic sourcing, for instance, links key purchasing decisions to a company's long-term competitive goals because it has a cross-organizational focus. This is normally associated with centralization. Strategic sourcing also calls for detailed, nuts and bolts knowledge of specific requirements and costs, which is a characteristic of decentralization.

Many companies now realize that a hybrid organizational structure with elements of both centralization and decentralization is the most efficient and effective corporate structure. One popular hybrid structure involves forming procurement councils comprised of personnel from multiple locations, including corporate headquarters and operating locations. These councils set the company's direction and priorities in line with the chief procurement officer's sourcing strategy. For material and service commodities that are commonly used, the procurement council forms cross-functional commodity teams on a priority basis.

These teams are led by a company representative with the most at stake for a particular commodity. This is generally the department that spends the most in a commodity category. For materials or services that fall outside traditional procurement areas, such as electricity, travel or benefits, procurement personnel usually become the key driver or team member, but they usually do not lead the team. The commodity team leader becomes an expert on the commodity and the focal point for communications with suppliers. As the commodity team sets supply relationships and contracts, the implementation and transactional functions, such as placing purchase orders, reverts to operating locations. Overall contracts are usually defined in broader terms, with individual locations defining their specific needs. The commodity team leader stays in close contact with the operating locations during implementation to ensure that the supplier is complying with the contract's requirements and that no recurring problems exist across multiple facilities.

7.2   Skills and Training

The next important internal component for implementing a strategic sourcing approach is the knowledge and skills of the sourcing personnel. Whether they are online purchasers or managers of large operations, individual staff members must have the appropriate skills to carry out sourcing for their goods. This will vary according to the quadrant in the sourcing model from which they operate. For instance, if purchasers are buying office supplies in the Automatic Pilot quadrant, then their skills will be far different than those needed for staff managing supply chain relationships in the high-value, high-need strategic partnership zone. Depending on the size of the company, staff may need to operate in more than one quadrant.

Undoubtedly, all staff must understand the strategic sourcing model if they want to prioritize their time and effort appropriately. They will also need the skill set required for each type of activity. Strategic sourcing means that procurement personnel can move quickly from undertaking mainly clerical duties to taking on a decision-making role. They are also involved in decisions across the organization. As a result, companies must invest heavily in retraining existing employees and, if necessary, recruiting personnel that have an expanded skill set that includes a background in both technical disciplines and advanced business degrees. Some of the skills required to carry out strategic sourcing are listed below:

Marketing and Strategic Analysis Strategic analysis skills are needed to identify the best suppliers, including those that may be outside the current industry. Buyers must be able to analyze and evaluate potential suppliers, perform constraint analyses, segment the supply market, pinpoint competition, analyze industry cost structures and understand pricing in accordance with a product's position in its lifecycle.

Information Gathering and Technical Knowledge Buyers also develop both relational and technical skills. Besides buying, they must continually seek information, learn about new materials and products, check for coherence and develop information networks outside the company.

Performance-Evaluation Skills In the past, price was the only way to evaluate suppliers. However, supplier-management techniques and cost-reduction practices have now made supplier evaluations more detailed. They include an assessment of services, co-development capacity, innovation ability, quality and lead-time accuracy.

Product-Development Skills Since they are at the forefront of the market and are responsible for costs, buyers are well placed to stimulate changes within a company. They must initiate joint development programs with suppliers on both products and services. Buyers must also comprehend value analysis and objective cost design, as well as identify opportunities to apply these techniques and propose product-enhancement pilot programs to technical staff.

Negotiation Skills and Partnership Development   In addition to day-to-day operation management skills, managing a partnership requires legal proficiency and negotiation skills. Once the partnership has been established, it is important to maintain and monitor the relationship.

7.3   Managing Suppliers and Partnerships

A broad spectrum of potential relationships exists between suppliers and purchasers under the strategic sourcing model, ranging from low-value, transaction-based interactions to partnerships that are high in strategic and financial value. As already discussed, companies that wish to adopt strategic sourcing should limit purchasing resources devoted to the lowest-value quadrant; most benefits can be derived from developing longer-term relationships with suppliers in the strategic partnership quadrant.

The strategic approach means that the traditional relationships pursued by buyers, suppliers and distributors must undergo a radical shake-up. In particular, the logic of the "zero-sum game" must be abandoned to escape the inherent opposition between players and competition among numerous suppliers. The win–lose mindset is replaced by the "win–win game" where cooperation and common goals take precedent. This strategy, which is naturally most applicable to the high-value strategic partnership zone, leads to preferential relationships with a limited number of suppliers.

A partnership relationship can be advantageous to both suppliers and purchasers when they adopt a "win–win" approach. Joint development of products and a continuous improvement program can improve products while reducing total costs, with both partners benefiting through a system where earnings are divided. When the competition is unable to match the relationship, the partners essentially benefit from a supplementary margin. It is important to shed any naïve thoughts regarding this type of partnership. Certainly it is based on mutual trust, but the equilibrium must be maintained through joint tracking of the partnership's performance to keep it going.

If the partnership falls into a state of disequilibrium of strengths between the players, the relationship would swing towards a zero-sum game. Several ways to maintain a partnership's equilibrium are outlined below.

First, the partnership must be defined clearly from the start. Contractual relations must guarantee an equitable division of effort and profit through the lifetime of the relationship. A rigorous definition of relations in the supplier/buyer contract is essential to achieving trade volume levels and stability. Precisely specifying the involvement of both parties in the relationship will minimize opportunistic behavior. If partnership's duration is well defined (the life of the product), then costs and service levels can be kept flexible and adjusted to take account of changes in consumer demand and internal process optimization, or indexed to raw material price levels. For example, a successful relationship contract will specify formulas for future price modifications, future distribution of productivity gains or supply chain cost enhancements.

Second, information must be transparent to both parties; the relationship's economic performance should be visible to all. At a high level, this involves the supplier's performance assessment, the quality of the buyer's demand forecast and the stability of technical specifications. Monitoring total procurement costs is also vital to a smooth relationship and often requires the classical controlling processes to be reorganized. Costs need to be distributed by supply units, with details not only on direct raw material and manpower costs, but also on indirect costs (such as logistics costs, non-quality costs and overhead).

The next level of visibility necessary for a long-lasting partnership focuses on the cost structures and profitability of both the supplier and buyer. Contractual agreements on price modifications and profit sharing require transparency on key performance indicators. The partnership remains competitive because its duration is fixed. To stay in business, suppliers must prove their competitiveness over the allocated time. Their cost structures are indicative of internal performance and can help guide enhancement and innovation initiatives.

Third, suppliers within a partnership should be evaluated on an enlarged performance basis, as discussed above under "performance-evaluation skills."

Fourth, partners should have the ability to initiate cost reductions, either through product redesign or by contributing to an integrated logistics strategy. Product design normally accounts for 40 % of an item's cost. Supply chain integration can also increase profits and creativity. As discussed above under "product development skills," change must be stimulated.

Finally, in addition to day-to-day management skills, managing a partnership requires legal proficiency and complex negotiation skills. Personnel skills will become even more important as buyers participate more in strategic business decisions.

7.4   Technology Enablers

The final key to the strategic sourcing model is information technology. By providing fast, direct links with supply chain partners, IT systems allow organizations to dramatically increase the amount of processed information and substantially reduce the amount of routine administrative effort required internally and across the supply chain. At almost every step of the purchasing process, technology has simplified repetitive tasks and provided greater capacity to gather and analyze critical information. At the planning stage, technology enables executives to forecast expenditure patterns. Once the transaction occurs, the data is captured and compared to the original forecast. As sourcing personnel start to analyze information concerning the use of products and services, IT can provide data about the organization's internal consumption patterns, as well as information about longer-term consumption trends and the factors driving demand. These systems also provide insight into the price, usage and process/administrative impacts of particular commercial deals.

When a firm is ready to go to market and choose suitable suppliers, online systems allow companies to collect information much more efficiently. Suppliers can provide online catalogues filled with product information that can be drilled into for specifications or viewed using easy-to-use point and click techniques. For large customers, suppliers can even provide custom-made catalogues that include pricing and availability information. For strategic sourcing personnel to gain a competitive advantage from their IT systems, they must be able to access an integrated suite of software applications called a "buyer's workstation." The workstation provides the best leverage when the underlying applications are interfaced with the company's internal purchasing and budgeting systems, and when the supply market can be accessed through the Internet. An Internet connection provides access to important data on industry trends and supply chain developments. It can also assist with supplier and product searches.

Technology makes it easier to receive spending approval and choose the correct account for the expense. Automatic routing for spending approval can be configured so that a request can be caught before the funds are committed. Identifying the expense early provides an opportunity to use procurement cards or other one-off, transaction-based payment systems. Procurement cards fit the model for miscellaneous consumption at this point.

IT also allows requests to be automatically consolidated into orders using the company's own application to consolidate product volumes. However, this function can be overridden if necessary to send approved orders without bundling. The technology can automatically release orders when the product, supplier, tax, logistics, approval and accounting requirements are all met.

Electronic communication such as electronic data interchange (EDI) minimizes the use of paper and reduces transaction costs while ensuring that the transaction occurs instantaneously. EDI can also transmit consumption forecasts to suppliers, enabling them to calibrate production for just-in-time delivery and obtain key performance data on every transaction record. At the same time, it's possible for an electronic funds transfer to pay for fully automated re-supply. For industrial companies, IT enables a firm and its suppliers to integrate production and supply. As new orders come in, each partner's supply chain and production cycle automatically jump into action. This integration simplifies the management of supplier relations, establishes long-term partnerships and shortens supply lead times.

Similarly in the retail industry, electronic interface and computer-aided communication allow products to be re-supplied automatically. This system, called continuous product replenishment (CPR), allows for the continuous update of sales/demand forecasts, the requirement for finished products and the issuance of purchase orders or transfer requests with scheduled deliveries. The integration of accounting functions is also simplified considerably. IT systems can release advance shipment notices (ASNs), which provide electronic information on products in transit. This assists the receiving warehouse in planning a shipment's arrival and in updating receipt records. Barcodes can further simplify the receiving process as workstations are set up to capture the coded information. This information can be used externally for supplier communication and internally for invoice processing, quality assurance and inventory availability.

Finally, in terms of payment, IT systems allow for auto-disbursement, which is set up based on evaluated receipt settlement. An exception base is built into the system to process mismatched transactions. Due to the use of electronic funds transfers for payment and automatic reconciliation from banking and financial institutions, in theory the buyer and supplier do not need to reconcile payments because this occurs automatically.

To ensure that technology is suited to strategic sourcing, the organization's business goals must drive the information technology systems and not vice versa. This requires a company to develop a separate information technology strategy that supports the strategic sourcing model. Links with channel partners through EDI or other Internet-based systems should be monitored periodically to ensure that they are actually improving the procurement performance.

Strategic Sourcing: Conclusion

The Future Is Now

Strategic sourcing is a new approach that promises to substantially improve an organization's competitiveness. Rather than adopting a singular, transaction-based method to procuring goods and services, strategic sourcing allows a company to identify the most appropriate sourcing method according to an item's importance to its overall business objectives. The most time and effort will be spent on items or contracts that offer the highest strategic and financial value. Strategic sourcing will continue to evolve, but companies that embrace the concept early will be well positioned to meet or exceed customer service demands and provide more price competitive products and services. Strategic sourcing will lower total costs for procurement, as well as improve product quality and service—ultimately boosting a company's competitive advantage.

It is no longer enough to focus simply on solving today's problems; the future is important now. Leaders need to anticipate and address potential opportunities, and adapt now to build a competitive edge. Though purchasing has changed from a vertical function of performing transactions to a highly integrative and strategic endeavor,[1] the field will continue to evolve in many ways:

- A purchaser's supplier base will continue to shrink and purchasing volume will continue to be consolidated across worldwide locations.
- More longer-term contacts will be awarded to selected suppliers with an increased effort to enhance their capabilities with joint activities and knowledge sharing.
- Procurement technology or sourcing tools such as e-procurement (various procurement portals designed to automate transactions from purchasing to payment, such as issuing purchase orders, automatic approval routing, delivery status

---

[1] William Atkinson, The Big Trends in Sourcing and Procurement, Supply Chain Management Review, May/June 2008.

© Springer Science+Business Media Singapore 2016
S. Parniangtong, *Supply Management*, Management for Professionals,
DOI 10.1007/978-981-10-1723-0

verification, invoicing and automation of payment) and e-sourcing (computer tools developed to facilitate the sourcing process such as e-RFI, reverse auction, e-auction, supplier selection and real-time negotiations) will continue to advance and make their way into core applications, including Enterprise Resource Planning (ERP).

- Web services will have a stronger influence on interactions between purchasers and suppliers. A great percentage of these interactions (like supplier performance management, real-time contract documentation, contract compliance, shipment status, advanced shipping notice and automated payment) will be web-based and many will happen transparently between systems.
- Global sourcing—seeking to procure materials from "low-cost" countries—will continue to grow from low-cost products with higher technology. The number of countries considered as sourcing candidates will also continue to increase.
- There will be an increasing number of companies outsourcing procurement oper-ations—transferring all or part of an organization's activities to a third party— with the objectives of:
  - Leveraging advanced technology
  - Centralization of operations for scale and scope of economies
  - Connecting to a larger base of suppliers

Successful leaders must address the above future-oriented trends and devote energy to identify today's necessary actions to meet future challenges and opportunities.

Index

© Springer Science+Business Media Singapore 2016
S. Parniangtong, *Supply Management*, Management for Professionals,
DOI 10.1007/978-981-10-1723-0

Made in the USA
Columbia, SC
13 November 2020